Rock Scars

James Hester

iUniverse, Inc.
New York Bloomington

Rock Scars

iUniverse books may be ordered through booksellers or by contacting:

iUniverse
1663 Liberty Drive
Bloomington, IN 47403
www.iuniverse.com
1-800-Authors (1-800-288-4677)

ISBN: 978-1-4401-2773-1 (pbk)
ISBN: 978-1-4401-2774-8 (ebk)

Printed in the United States of America

Library of Congress Control Number: 2009924291

iUniverse rev. date: 4/7/2009

Acknowledgements:

First, and always, I thank my favorite rock star Jesus Christ for helping me to live my life to the fullest daily. My wife Katie, the Hester, Atkinson, Nashel, Brady, and Henson families all have my appreciation for their love, support, and putting up with me and all of my loud music and mischief through the years. Special thanks to Barbara Arwood, Dr. Jim Schiavoni, and Dr. Curtis Chapman of Hiwassee College for helping me to become a better writer and for encouraging me to continue expressing myself. I can't thank Linda Garza enough for her support and her passion for helping others. She not only helped me become a counselor, she is a friend. Julie Jack-Warren is the embodiment of art. Thank you for listening without judgment, and for encouraging me to express myself in safe and healthy ways. I appreciate the staff and faculty at Tennessee Wesleyan College.

Thanks to all of the wonderful artists and musicians from Knoxville who have inspired me to never give up on my dreams and to be the best I can be. To James O' Neill, Brent & Shinedown, Gary Mitchell, shadowWax, AC Entertainment, Lenore Kinder, McGathy Promotions, In De Goot and Gwyther Bultman, Mel, 94.3 FM, Heidi Ellen Robinson Fitzgerald, Dr. Amy L. Skinner of UTK, The Daily Beacon, Paula Szeigis, Performer Magazine, The Knoxville Journal, Target Audience Magazine, and all of my peeps who believed in me and blessed me with so many wonderful experiences, thank you. Amy He at iUniverse rules!

To Harry & Bridgett Carroll, Don Moore, Jack Collins, and Master Jae Num Kim, thanks for being wonderful role models in my childhood. To Mike Bath, Jim McBrayer, Joe Sewell, and others in Oak Ridge who helped me, thank you. I thank the Church and its body for spiritual guidance and support. Front cover concept by Tim Hester. Cover photos by Katie Hester.

Preface

Much time, effort, and consideration has gone into writing this book in such a manner that I am understood and appreciated by both the entertainment industry and readers who otherwise may never do more than support entertainment. Thousands of thoughtful, heartfelt, hours were spent writing and preparing this book. To accurately report my experiences as a writer, and as a musician, is my sincere desire.

As an American supporting the rights to freedom of speech and freedom of the press, I ask that all persons named in this writing and photographed be graceful and to not take personal offense to the using of their names or faces. Words, phrases, and quotes attributed to persons named herein does not necessarily reflect any support or agreement from those persons with this author.

Many efforts have been made to verify all information contained in this publication. Many works are cited from this author's perspective, but all sources not cited, are the expressions of this author. The book you are reading reveals incites about an industry where "every rose has its thorn." During the process of researching and writing this piece, there were several delays and many changes along the way. Computers crashed, residences changed, employments changed, friends and family came and went. Editors and publishers were sought and deals were negotiated. Hopefully, readers will be inspired to shine like stars and not to painfully fade away like scars.

Contents

AUTOBIOGRAPHY INTRO...

Marshall Mathers. My, my, my... Regardless of what I like or dislike about the guy, I have to admit he sells himself well. I'm not really giving him props, but I think he's a perfect example of entertainment marketing. Why? Like anyone else in the business, he learned early on that you gotta have a game plan. Call it a gimmick or whatever, but the man believed in himself when no one else would. He has a lot of courage and charisma. I respect that. I might not have lived in the same circumstances, but I can relate well with a poor white boy whom people called "trash" and said would amount to nothing. Those who know me well know that I wasn't always the ambitious young gentleman who graduated college with honors. Let me share with you a little of how I can relate with Eminem...

Similar to Marshall, I've had to overcome some obstacles in my rise to fame and fortune. We both grew up in an era when racism was more accepted as "the norm," and had to struggle to overcome poverty and other curses inherited from previous generations. During the course of this writing, I had setbacks that might have made many folks give up, if they had faced similar circumstances. I struggled with the stigma and limitations that often come with having a disability, because I have paralysis and a large scar on my left arm. Like Eminem, I battled in adolescence to function well in spite of living with a dysfunctional family.

I experienced more turnover in my employment during the course of this writing than I had planned. In 2005, I was involved in a terrible auto accident that left me physically unharmed, but emotionally scarred, as I witnessed firsthand the death of a man in another vehicle. No one involved was charged with a crime. However, it left me with a renewed appreciation for life, plus an opportunity to finish this book. People can only begin to imagine the many sleepless nights that I've had and the tears and pain that I've poured into the heartfelt story you are reading. I have talked about this treasured literary ambition for what has seemed like half of eternity. I hate to simply talk and not follow through on things. It was my intention to have completed this tale long ago, but nature and time chose differently. For me, "this is the moment." This is my opportunity that only comes "once in a lifetime." I've never met Eminem, prior this writing, but I gained a better understanding and respect for him after seeing his movie *8 Mile*.

My story began in the hills of East Tennessee, growing up mostly in a time and place with two kinds of people: Black and White. I was born at St. Mary's, a private Catholic hospital in Knoxville. I'm named after my dad's younger brother who also was born there, but died shortly afterwards. My parents weren't Catholic, but preferred good private hospitals to public ones, plus my mom used to work there when she was a teenager. Before my parents separated, and soon later divorced, I lived in mostly-White communities.

After my parents separated when I was ten, I moved with my mom and brothers to a poorer section of town. We moved there to live with my maternal grandmother, because we had little to no support from my father. My father loved us and meant well, but for reasons I may never know or fully understand, he was not a stable source of support. Of course, we lied about our home address. My mother would leave home an extra hour earlier in the mornings to drive my brothers and me to schools in better neighborhoods where most of our friends were. My mother wanted the best for us. She wanted us to play on the best ball teams, be in the best Boy Scout troops, and go to the best schools.

The house on Oklahoma Avenue was a shabby, old, green house on the corner. I think it was built in the 1930s. At any rate, it was about 50 years old. It had a small little area of grass that was far from being a yard like the previous homes we were accustomed to. The city's sidewalk wasn't far from the front porch and door. Along with my mother, brothers, and I all staying together in one bedroom, there was my mom's mother who would either migrate between that house and the one down the street with her husband Harold, my mom's stepdad.

She would usually just sleep on the couch in the living room, if she chose to stay overnight. It was kinda weird. My maternal grandmother is a wonderful woman, but in those days she drank a lot, and my brothers and I often saw her drunk. Throughout my childhood, whenever I saw my grandma, she usually had a bottle of bourbon with her. Thankfully, the prayers of family, friends, and myself were answered and God delivered my grandmother from alcoholism. She has been sober for over five years now. I am so proud of her. She has always been someone I have admired and looked up to.

My mom's mother raised eight children. My mother is the oldest, but her father died when she was just about four years old. He was also an alcoholic. Sadly, I am told that he drank himself to death, and was only about 34 years old when he died. Growing up, my mother and her siblings always thought that my grandmother just remarried when my grandfather died. That's also what I was told during my childhood. However some research recently found that my grandmother actually divorced my granddad before marrying Harold. It makes sense. According to stories from my mother that grandma used to tell her, my grandpa was a mean, raging, type of alcoholic. I was told that he was often violent and used to hurt my grandmother. So, although divorce was taboo in those days, my grandmother ended the violence, thus protecting herself and my mother.

Anyhow, there were a total of three bedrooms. One bedroom housed my mom's younger sister Germaine and her boyfriend, plus their kids. The other room housed my mom's younger brother Mark, his girlfriend, and their kids. It was an interesting arrangement to say the least. We had just one bathroom in the old house. It had one of those antique, white, porcelain tubs that sat on four legs, plus a shower that would turn cold whenever anyone else used the toilet and flushed, or used water in another part of the house. The bathroom had a small, white, porcelain sink that hung from the wall with the pipes coming out of the wall underneath it. The sink had those lovely, old-fashioned, metal handles that one would turn like a wheel.

I think the way we managed to share is that every bedroom had its own sort of unwritten schedules. Using the bathroom got kinda crazy sometimes. That same house is where I had pneumonia for the first time. One morning I woke up and my lips were swelled up three times their normal size and were purple. I got scared and cried. I ended up going to Children's Hospital that day instead of school. It's a good thing I did, because I had bacterial pneumonia and an intestinal infection. It was a bit traumatic for me as a kid. I don't think I've ever puked as much and as often as I did then in my entire life. I got better after a week in the hospital being fed through IVs.

That house got cold in the winter, the floors, especially. There was a draft that went through the house. It must not have been insulated much, because it turned into an oven in the summer. There was, however, one cool thing about living there. It was the wailing, heavy-metal thunder of my uncle Mark jamming on his guitar! He was one of the first people in my life to introduce me to the power of ROCK n' ROLL!!! He jammed some great classics. He could play the cool stuff by bands like Van Halen, Tom Petty & The Heart Breakers, Iron Maiden, Lynyrd Skynyrd, Black Sabbath, The Police, The Cars, and of course... KISS!!! Uncle Mark ruled. He was always good with kids. He also had the coolest straight, long hair. We were always taught by our parents that boys shouldn't have long hair, so naturally, we loved uncle Mark. He was our hero, a true "rock n' roll rebel." Where was I? Oh yeah!

The house had high ceilings, uncarpeted hardwood floors, and had an infestation of mice, roaches, rats, and ants. Hey, the cats loved that house! There was an unsecured building beside it that we used to store some things in. I'll never forget the day I went to get my really rad bicycle out of that building only to find that it had been stolen. I cried and wept bitterly. I wasn't as upset at the bike being stolen as I was at where I was living, which ultimately was the reason in my young mind. I know now that theft can happen anywhere, not just in the ghetto.

So, it wasn't long that we lived with my maternal grandmother before my mother, brothers, and I moved back to "the good section" of Knoxville. In fact, we moved four times before we settled in Oak Ridge where my brothers and I all finished high skull. After living with grandma, we first moved into a small house on a hill off of Western Avenue, located in the Cumberland Estates Community. It was a house beside the church where my brother Robert and I would walk over to Boy Scout meetings, plus to a shopping center with an arcade, or to a convenient store also in the neighborhood. Cumberland Estates was a nice neighborhood. It was suburbia.

We didn't worry about much in those days as kids, because a lot of our friends and school peers lived in that same neighborhood. Plus there were lots of nosey, concerned parents living there in Cumberland Estates. It was also where the coolest skateboarder I've ever known lived. His name was Robert Taylor, but local kids called him Ret, an acronym for Robert Edward Taylor. Ret was a few years older and he and his sister Lisa lived in the house behind us. They went to a local private school called Webb.

They had to wear uniforms to school. Ret was about 16 or 17 when we met and he drove himself to school. He was really cool to us younger kids. I remember the day we met. He had a customized launch ramp that he made himself. It stayed outside his carport leaned up against the wall. It had wheels on one end so it could be moved easily. Imagine a wooden ramp that looked sort of like a triangular wedge. When we met one day, Ret was being a cool, "skater dude," in his carport. We were walking along through his yard, like any thoughtless youths would, and saw him doing tricks on his board and using the ramp.

My brother Robert was with me and we were like "Wow man! Check that guy out!" Life in suburbia wasn't like when my brothers and I lived "in the hood" on Oklahoma in north Knoxville. After living behind Ret for about three years, my hopes and dreams were once again shattered (adolescence). My brothers, our mother, and myself were all forced to move again! The house we lived in was going to be sold for some sort of doctor's office, or something, so we had to go!

I had planned on getting to start high skull with all of the childhood friends I grew up with, including my best bud Rob Collins, at West High! No! "How could this evil have come upon me?" I thought to myself. I had already gone to a party at Mr. Gilbert's (West High Band Director) house, and had met some cool kids I was going to be in band with! What's worse is that I knew some cute girls at West, but I knew NOBODY at Central. West was best! It was a school full of "rednecks and hoods," and Central was a sucky school full of "preps and jocks!" *grin* I asked the question "WHY?" many times.

This second move prior to Oak Ridge landed me at Pine Ridge Apartments. As much as I wanted to go to West, I couldn't because I was no longer "zoned" for that school district. So, I grudgingly went to Central. Before my parents divorced, I rarely saw Black kids living in the same neighborhood I did. Latinos, Asians, and others lived in some part of the world far away from my little Caucasian utopia. It wasn't until 1991, my second freshman year in high skull, that Knox County decided to desegregate public schools by busing poor Black students and teachers from the inner-city to mostly-White schools in the suburbs. It was a tumultuous time due to the rise of racism under the guise of cultural pride and ethnocentrism.

The year 1992 brought me to a town, just outside of Knoxville, called Oak Ridge. At the time, it was way better than Knoxville. Oak Ridge, Tennessee had a better economy, better schools, and more job opportunities at that time. Plus, it was still a small town with a more-personal ambiance than K-Town. My mother, brothers, and I moved to Oak Ridge because she wanted to be closer to her boyfriend, who eventually became my stepdad. Mom got a job there so she could be closer to him… Joy…

Okay, to clarify, at that time I was a typical self-centered teenage boy who disrespected his single mother and gave her a tough time. It didn't take long for me and my mom's man to "lock horns." We first moved to Oak Ridge in the same apartment community he lived in. I had been a carefree teen with the absence of a male authority figure to give me direction and help me to be more respectful towards my mother and others. To me, he was just some washed up Army-vet who suffered from PTSD. At that time, he was just some dude scheming on my mom who wanted to become "mein fürher." Thankfully, time and faith helped us get to know each other better. We've both grown and become better individuals. Now, he, my mom, and I have a good, close relationship with each other. Nowadays, I embrace diversity and try to respect everyone.

Oak Ridge was a good experience for me though. My mom,

brothers, and I moved out of that nice apartment community, where my stepdad lived, and into another growing experience. We moved into some government subsidized housing. Yeah!!! Yep, we moved into the PROJECTS. I look back on it now and laugh. It really wasn't that bad. The subsidized apartments we moved to were pretty new, only about a year old, and better still was that they were not located in a section of Oak Ridge known as "The Valley." So, what was wrong with The Valley? It was told to me on TV, and by other kids at Oak Ridge High, that it was not a place where White folks were welcome.

With that in my mind, I wondered and asked myself "So, what about the projects where I live? What's going to happen here?" I came to discover that living there at Van Hicks Apartments really wasn't that bad. Sure, it was mostly Black people living there, but I didn't get into any trouble with my neighbors. Occasionally, I would hear "Hey white boy!" or "Hey cracker!", but it wasn't a common occurrence. Routinely, there would be drug dealers roll into the community in "Benzos, Caddies, Beemers, or tricked-out hoopties," but I'd just pick up the phone and call the apartment manager, or when things got noisy, I'd call the cops. I mostly just kept to myself. I didn't talk to neighbors, unless they spoke to me first.

The same proved to be true in the mornings on my way to school. Sometimes, I was the only White boy on the bus. Every morning my school bus would pick me and other kids up at Van Hicks and would take us to where I had been told I shouldn't go: THE VALLEY. Well, guess what? I never got shot, stabbed, beat up, or picked on by any of the kids from THE VALLEY. Only once did a Black kid disrespect me by repeatedly saying "Hey, white boy." It got on my nerves, but I stayed cool, and I never saw that kid again. Further, before moving out of Oak Ridge in 1994, I used to give a Black friend "Boo-Boo" a ride home from work late at night. Where did he live? You guessed it! He lived in The Valley. So, Oak Ridge helped me learn not to have my thoughts captivated by stereotypes. However, there was a riot in The Valley once, and some White cops were killed.

Genuinely caring about people is very important to me. What color you are, where you're from, how much money you have, or what your gender is concerns me less. We might not share the same faith, religion, or philosophy, but you are still valuable. Sure, I respect some folks more than others, but we can co-exist. Oak Ridge was more diverse a place than any I had previously lived because scientists and others from all over the world lived there for their jobs in the nuclear facilities. Oak Ridge was planned, and built, by the federal government in the 1940s, mostly for the purpose of manufacturing and assembling nuclear weapons. I'll share my thoughts on that in another time and place...

Anyways, living in Oak Ridge was cool. My high skull experience was a much happier one there than in Knoxville. My first three years of high skull were vomit. My last year was spent at Oak Ridge. The kids in Oak Ridge were generally more mature and better behaved, plus I seemed to fit in with them more easily. There were still cliques at Oak Ridge High, but most of the different subgroups within the academic culture there seemed to co-exist well. The high skull I attended in Knoxville was saturated with separatist-groupie mentalities. Everyone, including the teachers, seemed to be having a personal identity crisis.

My teen years were much like an old song called *Subdivisions*, by the rock band Rush. It was a matter of "Be cool, or be cast out." I'm very happy no longer being a depressed and antisocial kid wallowing in my insecurities. Confidence and comfort with myself became a part of me after high skull, and especially college. It wasn't until my master's degree program at the University of Tennessee that I began to be more aware of my own feelings and actions.

During my college days in Tennessee, I was sort of a "rock star" writing for newspapers and magazines, and meeting several celebrities. Playing trumpet and singing helped me earn that title also. I won some awards along the way...craved attention, drove a gold 735i BMW, was arrogant, and was a "social butterfly." I bragged about my grades and who knew me. So, I really was a rock star right? Who cares!?! To this day, I'm sorry for having behaved that way. I still want to be appreciated, and sometimes recognized, but please don't label me a "rock star."

Smirk Anyhow, let's back up and start with my childhood years and how I was inspired to become a celebrity. The first popular person I remember meeting (ok, for a kid he was big time) was the Black, bald-headed guy from the TV show Sesame Street. It was Roscoe Orman! Shopping with my mom and brothers at West Town Mall, of course I spotted him walking along. Whoah... The bald brotha from Sesame Street! Ok. Insert laughter here. The guy was really cool. It was even more cool than getting to meet Santa Claus, especially since Saint Nick was fake. He stopped and spoke with us, and shook hands. Groovy.

The next great celebrity I got to meet was the NFL's "Minister of Defense," Reggie White. Reverend Reggie played football for the University of Tennessee during my childhood. We met on a field trip in first grade at a theme park called Silver Dollar City. Country music diva Dolly Parton later bought that theme park and developed it into Dollywood. Reggie, like me, was (R.I.P) a Tennessee boy. Dolly, like myself, is also from the hills. She is from the Smoky Mountains just east of Knoxville. I would later in life hang out with Dolly's producer Scottie Hoglan at a recording studio in Knoxville, but I'll get back to that later...

Like many kids, I wanted to be a baseball player when I grew up. I wanted to be like Johnny Bench and Pete Rose. The "Big Red Machine" was my team! Of course, they inspired me to play baseball. A TV show used to come on with Cincinnati Reds catcher Johnny Bench and Montreal Expos catcher Gary Carter as the hosts. Johnny and Gary would have little, average kids come on the show and they would demonstrate to those kids some of the mechanics and techniques of good baseball playing. Gary and Johnny were my heroes. I still have old baseball cards of them. I also own a biography of Johnny Bench that I found when I was about nine years old. It's titled *From Behind the Plate*. I lugged that book to school on reading days and read it cover to cover about four times. My ball glove was a Gary Carter signature series, when I played catcher. Anyhow, those guys helped me and many other kids believe in themselves.

Sometime in either the fourth or fifth grade, my class took a field trip and I got to meet Johnny Cash at the Museum of Appalachia in Norris, Tennessee. All I remember was meeting a tall man dressed in black who had a deep voice. It really wasn't that exciting, because I didn't know who the guy was. Recognizing the Dukes of Hazard would have been easy, but at that time, Johnny was just some nice man people said was famous. Mr. Cash wasn't as cool as the Muppets then, but now I love Johnny!

In the fifth grade I played baseball on a team that included future Olympic track and field pro Tony Cosey. I was the mediocre kid who played left field. I forget which position Tony played, but he could smoke the bases with his running speed. He was a year or two older than me, and we spoke some when we both attended North West Middle Skull. Northwest was also where football player Reggie White went to middle school some years prior to me. His aunt, Mrs. Upton was my English teacher there. I was mostly a trendy follower during my middle school years. I didn't understand that it was cool to just be yourself and be genuine. I wanted to have long hair and get chicks like the band Def Leppard..."Pour some sugar on me!!!" Being a "hood" was my ambition. When I arrived at Central High Skull, I had the opportunity to play ball with Tony again, along with future major-leaguers Bubba Trammell and Todd Helton. Bubba played for the Detroit Tigers after high skull and Todd played for the Colorado Rockies. Todd's uncle Joel Helton was my

World Geography teacher. Joel also worked as a coach for the football and baseball teams at Central High.

Several friends tried to get me to tryout for Central High's baseball team. Joel Helton even encouraged and asked me to tryout, but like many rock stars during their teen years, I was depressed. I battled depression, alcoholism, low self- esteem, and personal insecurity during my adolescent years. I was a wreck. All I wanted to do then was the usual angst-filled living of a depressed kid. I hated to go to school, and made it a point to miss as often as I could get away with. I hated other kids and they hated me was my thought.

Like a lot of kids, I just wanted to fit in and be accepted when I attended Central. I was trying to find myself. True to my musical roots, I listened to pretty much "a little of everything" while I was at Central --but, especially hard music by bands like Black Sabbath, Anthrax, Slayer, Carcass, Death, Metallica, Public Enemy, Danzig, Suicidal Tendencies, Minor Threat, Ministry, Prong, Coroner, Testament, Megadeth, Dead Kennedys, Rollins Band, Misfits, Sepultura, and Exploited... I lived in a more-desolate reality and those groups of musicians shared that with me it seemed.

Following in the lead of my role models Gun's 'N Rose, Alice in Chains, and Ozzy Osbourne, I checked into the adolescent treatment facility at St. Mary's, the hospital where I was born--AGAIN!!! It was ironic. The place that helped with my birth, also was the place that helped with my rebirth. I'm not talking about my faith or religion, but those found me later. I made a complete turnaround with my life. I had to compromise- not with my integrity, but with my ego. Accepting the fact that I might have been wrong a time or two (ok, more times than I care to count), I had to swallow my pride. Before therapy, I rebelled against myself. After I got help, anyone or anything that might bring me harm became an enemy.

After finishing treatment at age 17, I wanted more out of life. Before St. Mary's assisted me, I lacked ambition. I never finished anything I started, unless it was a good drink (ok any drink). I dropped out of high school, quit playing trumpet, and stopped listening to my parents. I quit Boy Scouts. My Christian faith ended. I quit martial arts training. My skateboarding ceased. I decided back in October 1992 that failure wasn't going to be my legacy. As a reward for my progress and completing treatment, my mother let me go to see rock 'n roll legend Ozzy Osbourne live in concert. It was supposed to be his last show ever in Knoxville, because Ozzy had announced his retirement. It was called the "*No More*

Tours, Tour." Sepultura and Alice In Chains opened for Ozzy at that event.

Whether he realizes it or not, Ozzy was a big inspiration for my sobriety. I thought "If Ozzy can get sober and make music, I can." During my time in rehab, the sales pitch to my mom was that Ozzy had kicked several habits and had gained control over his life. I convinced mom that Ozzy had "cleaned up." Mr. Osbourne was now a safe form of entertainment. No more bats or birds dying for the wrath of PETA! Sharon and Ozzy were "flying high again!" Sadly, it was only a short time after I saw Ozzy in concert that he relapsed completely. He even went so far as to say in interviews and advertisements that "sobriety sucks!" I still appreciate his music and humor, but I am disappointed in Ozzy having chosen to use his substance abuse as a clever marketing tool.

However, in a 2007 interview with Fox TV's Greta Van Sustern, Ozzy claimed he was sober, and for the first time in all of the years I had seen him on TV, Ozzy actually looked and sounded the most sober he had ever been. His speech was not the usual delayed slurs and stutters he was known for on his reality TV show *The Osbournes*. Ozzy was relaxed, yet articulate and intelligent. I'm proud of him. Hopefully, he can maintain his sobriety this time. I want him to still be performing when he's 100 years old, so I can take my grandkids to see the real "Wizard of Oz." It'll be an event with me telling the grandkids something like: "Hey kids, you think your grandpa's a crazy old fart, check this guy out!"

I'm not picking on Ozzy. I remember in Metallica's earlier years the band had a t-shirt which read on its front "Alcoholica... 100% Proof." I love Metallica and Ozzy, and I know they've grown and matured a lot since then. Even though I disagree with those advertisements, I can't try to pass any judgments on anyone, because I know, without anyone having to tell me, that I have said and done plenty of controversial things. Oh well...At least I had a job to go back to after my rehab. I returned to being a greasy-faced teen being exploited by the golden arches as a form of cheap, high-quality labor. Ok...ok... We all gotta start somewhere right? Overall, working in fast-food like most teens was actually a good experience. It was good to learn about how some folks have to work just to get by. It was terrible to just exist and live from pay-check to pay-check, which several of my coworkers did. Working in a fast-food restaurant gave me an incentive to get my education and to do more with my life. That's, just me.

Some folks actually like fast-food, or at least make a career out of it. I remember one of my store managers named Roy. We started working together in 1992. When I transferred from my golden experience in

Knoxville to the one in Oak Ridge, Roy had already worked for the company since 1964. When I moved out of Oak Ridge in 1994, he was still the manager! I remember him well… He was a bald-headed White guy with a mustache and side burns. He was about average weight and five feet tall. The guy smoked like a chimney and drank coffee like a filter. He had a class ring where he had gone to college on a company scholarship to the "Hamburger University."

Wow! How could anyone have that much ambition and work that hard I thought? When Roy ran the place, he could and would work circles around anybody. Fast-food and culinary school wasn't my scene or dream, but I totally respect the guy. He had a passion for his work. Laugh, but his ambition actually inspired mine. We just chose different paths –different careers to follow. I still work in serving the public as an educator, and like Roy, I care about people. Roy cared enough then to hire a bunch of kids and give them chances. It seemed like he hired every high skull kid at some point.

Other folks might call me a smoocher, but I wasn't then and I'm not now. You should remember where you've been and give respect to the "old-school." There was also a manger named Becky (I think that was her name) who seemed to care about folks, even though she was usually stressed at work. I remember getting out of the hospital and coming back to work with them and they were so supportive. I didn't get paid much and only got a ten-cent raise after being there a year, but at least the folks were good to work with.

My last year of high school finally came in 1993. As I said before, Oak Ridge High was pretty cool, but rather than become a fifth-year senior, I wanted out! So, I got my GED. After not getting along with my mom and stepdad, I moved out and got my own apartment shortly before they were married. So, unlike my brothers, I never resided with my stepdad in the same house. I started studies at a two-year technical college in Knoxville called Pellissippi State. In the fall of '93, I took just Developmental Math and English Comp. to get started.

Working full-time and doing college part-time, is how I could afford the grandiose lifestyle of a poor 18 year-old guitarist. As singer/shock-rock pioneer Alice Cooper put it, I couldn't tell if I was a boy, or if I was a man. "Like it! Love it! Eighteen!!!" Like a little bird let out of a cage, upon moving into my first apartment, I quickly flew away from the nest. I wasn't always mature enough to handle it. It was at that time when I discovered the "night life." Accepting the smooth ambiance a young man yearns for, I found a place where I finally felt like I fit in –it was *The Underground.* I had finally arrived. Amidst the darkness, strobe-lights, and antique furnishings of what used to be an old warehouse, I found camaraderie with the alter natives.

My musical influences and compositions began to be more experimental after beginning my nocturnal journey. In 1993 and '94 the scene began to bust wide open with technological improvisations that made dance floors everywhere shake with earthquake rhythms. The Internet was in its genesis and synthetic sounds allowed average Joes to become maestros. Those years introduced me to such artists as Al Jourgensen, Lords of Acid, KMFDM, Prodigy, Moby, BIGOD 20, Godflesh, Us3, Fear Factory, Kraftwerk, and German pioneers Einstreuzende Neubauten. I still have a nifty Kawai keyboard that my dad's best friend Gerant gave me and I spent countless hours experimenting as a result of those influences.

To support my newly-found freedom, I quit fast-food to work for a classy new restaurant in town called the *Mustard Seed Café*. I worked in the kitchen mostly preparing food, but also stocking and cleaning. They paid and treated me pretty well. The Mustard Seed was where I met my first real girlfriend, because Jennifer was the first girl I ever really had a long-term relationship with. She was a great friend. The *Mustard Seed Café* was where my good friends Ben and Lorie worked too.

The Mustard was a good place to work, but it stayed busy. It was the first job I had after moving out on my own. I will never forget as long as I live coming into work one evening, just to check my schedule, and hearing my friend Ben Savage ask me if I had heard. "Heard what?" He said "Kurdt Cobain's dead." "Ah, bull! That's not funny!" I said. With a slated, sullen look on his face, Ben put a hand on each of my shoulders, looked me straight in the eyes and said grimly "I'm not lying to you bro." No, it wasn't true. It had to be a cruel rumor I thought.

This wasn't Elvis, it was Kurdt the king of *my* musical inspiration. How could it be? I didn't want to believe it. I went straight home after finding out and turned on MTV. Kurt Loder was breaking the news as I began to weep. I rarely cry, but that day I shed some tears. *Nirvana* was a huge influence on my life as well as my music. I lit up a cigar, started sippin' on "8-Ball," grabbed my acoustic, tuned to D, and softly started strumming "Hey! Wait! I've got a new complaint…"

A short time later, I quit the Mustard Seed and moved to tiny Englewood, Tennessee to live with my dad's mother and his brother, plus go to college. Two traffic lights and 1200 citizens… They "knowed" this city boy wasn't from around there. Twang wasn't my thang, and it was obvious. I had not planned on living in Englewood, or with my dear, sweet, grandmother permanently, but things change… About two weeks after I moved there and began to enjoy the serenity of rural living, tragedy struck. I was on my way to Oak Ridge to jam with my high school buds Matt Hall and Aaron Armour. Both were, and still are, incredible musicians. Matt was going to be spastic on bass that day and I was scheduled to provide the "hypro glow" on my guitar. Aaron had planned on having his usual prodigy of rhythm on drums. We would've worked out the vocals had I made it to our session.

That morning, on my way to Oak Ridge, my car collided with a transfer truck and I very nearly lost my life. Thankfully, I was sober and I had learned while I was in an adolescent treatment unit, the year prior, to deal with the emotions and events of my life in a healthy manner. No one involved was charged with a crime or found guilty of one. I was unconscious and in a coma for about three weeks. Miraculously, my rare Gibson survived the wreck, but my old Ampeg amplifier was destroyed. Thankfully, I left my acoustic guitar, my trumpet, and my keyboard at home that day.

Ultimately, that sad event changed my life forever, but it made me a better and stronger person. As a result, my career as a musician had to temporarily be placed on standby. My left arm was very nearly amputated and it sustained permanent paralysis due to severe radial nerve damage. To this day, I don't know if I will ever be able to play guitar as well as I did prior to that accident. Thankfully, I have found other ways to express myself through music, and also other ways to enjoy it.

So, I may not ever be the next Joe Satriani, but on trumpet, I can really blow!!! *grin* I am thankful everyday that I have my trumpet to return to. I may not ever play trumpet as well as I played guitar, but I'm fine with it. What matters more is to still have an instrument I can become so mesmerized and in love with that my mind and soul are magically transported through time and space to a better place and a higher reality. Music is a gift. Therefore, I enjoy the present. Hallelujah!!!

I made do the best I could, but never really felt completely accepted by the locals in the seven years living in Englewood. However, I haven't forgotten the kindness and support of the church and the locals when my dad died, and also when my grandmother died. Most people there were good and decent, but they were more shy to outsiders than I preferred. As a writer and musician, I'm not shy. I learned when I started playing trumpet at age nine that it is sometimes necessary to open up and be a little more vulnerable than usual. I went through a phase in my teenage years of being withdrawn and introverted.

I used to be the skinny little White guy that came to school dressed in either all black, or only black and white. The all black generally reflected my mood and the philosophies I respected during that time.

The black and white combination came after I embraced Daoism and Asian philosophies. I used to wear a ring that was Sterling-silver and had a yen-yang inlaid on the top. I wasn't going to graduate from high school, so it was like a graduation present to myself. Years later, I returned to being a Christian, but I still continue to learn about other faiths and philosophies.

After living in Englewood for seven years with my dear, sweet, grandmother, I moved back to the city I grew up in, Knoxville, to pursue my master's degree at the University of Tennessee. I had planned on moving out after I graduated college, but originally thought I would go to either Vanderbilt, Duke, or Emory University to work on my master's degree. The "Big Orange" made me an offer I couldn't refuse. After UT offered me a full-tuition scholarship with a stipend for monthly living expenses, I knew I would head back to "Knox Angeles." Still having a disability, Vocational Rehabilitation Services paid for my housing while I worked on my master's degree. It was all sort of surreal. My prayers were answered. It was "a long strange trip" trucking through academia, but it was very cool. I went from having been a high school dropout to having earned a master's degree. Wow. Success rocks!

Now I am compelled to ask myself the question: "What is success?" Every individual person has his or her own unique definition of what success is or isn't. I have found in my years of playing music and journalistic writing that what an individual artist might perceive to be a successful piece of work can be perceived by the industry as a pile of poo, and vice versa. I worked hard and made good grades in college, but still felt that by society's standards I was a failure. I felt like a failure because after I earned my master's degree I still had a lot of difficulty finding a good paying job.

The job I thought I was going to get working for the State of Tennessee as a vocational rehabilitation counselor fell through, because the governor placed a freeze on the hiring in order to balance Tennessee's budget and economy. As a result, I could no longer afford to front in my gold BMW 735i. I was forced to sell my sweet "Beamer" and drive "my work car," my 1987 Pontiac Grand Am. It didn't rock the road like my BMW did, and in my mind, it was a chick repellent. Of course, I now know and understand that I was just really insecure and shallow for awhile, because I wanted people to like me. It was just a facade.

I even ended up moving in with one of my mother's church friends and living for a short time in her basement, because my "rock star" budget was so screwed up! Further, while living in that basement I found a job working at Walmart as a cashier for $6.50 and hour! With a MASTER'S degree! However, some money was better than no money. Actually, I really enjoyed that job. The management and my coworkers were great to work with and I got to meet many interesting people who came through my check-out lane. It was easy work. Being always friendly and sociable, I would say hello to all of my customers and try to chat with them a little. It was there where I first learned by mass numbers of customers that I bore some sort of resemblance to actor Edward Norton from "that movie Fight Club."

Maybe, after I am rich and famous from the writing and sales of this book, I'll go back to work as a cashier at Walmart, so people can walk up to me thinking I'm Ed Norton and ask me for my autograph! Of course, I'd tell them that I'm not a famous actor, but then I'd have the opportunity to tell them about a great book called *Rock Scars* that I'm mentioned in heh...heh... Two months after working at Walmart I got hired by the Georgia Department of Labor to be a vocational rehabilitation counselor. I have lived in Georgia ever since and that is ultimately where I was blessed to find my beautiful and wonderful wife Katie. She has been a huge inspiration and source of support for this book! I thank God for allowing me the experiences I had during college and the years following up to this book. It was a long and challenging road to follow, but it helped me shine a little brighter.

CHAPTER ONE

Horse Sense

My uncle, David Hester, has a good friend Keith who is an awesome guitarist. I used to hang out with Keith and my uncle prior to my moving to Englewood. Keith, or "Ham" as most folks called him, was a long-haired white guy who looked sorta like an overweight version of Ted Nugent from the VH-1 show *Supergroup*. With his straw hat and ragged attire, Keith constantly surprised me with how smart he really was, in spite of his appearance. He would jam some great classic rock with me, stuff by Lynyrd Skynyrd, Jimi Hendrix, Crème, Molly Hatchet, AC/DC, and of course Ted Nugent.

He would also discuss really deep issues with (okay, anything is deep when you're a teenager) me like sociology, Native American history, or psychoanalysis and how Sigmund Freud's cocaine use helped inspire many to try the drug. Anyhow, one day he told me something I'll never forget. He said: "James, none of America's politicians are worth spit anymore. They're all educated idiots. I'll take a man with good 'ol fashioned horse sense any day over a man with a wall full of college degrees, who don't know about average people. What good is a college degree, if you can't find your way out of a paper bag?" I never forgot Keith's sense of modern Renaissance wisdom, and indeed always made it a point from there on to try and relate well with all kinds of people.

From the time I started writing for my first 'zine *The Rag Muffin*, an underground project I published in 1998, I have gained a lot of horse sense about journalism and writing about the entertainment industry. I learned that there are certain rules of etiquette for writers and always codes of ethics that one has to establish in the writing process. I learned simply to have good manners and to always be considerate of whom or what I am writing about. I also learned to write in the "third person," during my college composition courses. I learned when I started writing for *The Daily Beacon Newspaper* that most journalistic writing is done in a style established by the Associated Press called AP Style. I felt so completely ignorant when I initially learned this, because my first 'zine the *Rag Muffin* was written in the MLA style, and so was the first issue of my second and more-serious effort, *The Vüe Magazine*. Purchasing an

AP writer's handbook from a university bookstore is something else I did while in graduate school, and it has benefited my writing style.

Since this book is about becoming a "rock star," and the scars one acquires in the process, the term should be defined. A rock star is any appreciated person who has obtained frequent attention, respect, or fame as a result of his or her appearance, ideals, or actions. According to that definition, it is not necessary for one to be a musician in order to be a rock star. That would make President Obama, Elvis, The Pope, Kermit the Frog, Keaneau Reeves, or local high school homecoming queens all rock stars. Like the previously mentioned celebrities, one has to have a great amount of horse sense, or at least work with others who do, in order to be a rock star.

Rock stars have the responsibility of constantly being in the public eye, along with enduring the pressure of being expected to always perform well. I witnessed evidence of this firsthand in the before and after activities of my friend Brent Smith and the band he sings with, Shinedown. I saw Shinedown for the band's first performance in Knoxville at the popular music club Blue Cats. Upon arrival at the venue, I walked over to the band's tour bus, parked outside the building.

After walking the sidewalk between the bus and the backdoor of the club's stage, I knocked on the bus door. A few seconds later, a black-haired young lady wearing a black t-shirt with the word "FILTH" printed boldly in white on the front (she was a fan of the band Cradle of Filth), and snuggly accenting her curves, pranced down the steps and out the door to greet me. "Hey! What's up?" she asked. I introduced myself and explained that I had known Brent for a few years, and I used to write about his previous band Dreve. I handed her my business card: "James Hester, Arts & Entertainment Journalist" and asked her to tell him I was at the show. She said "Sure. Hold on. I'll tell him."

A few seconds later the bus began to rumble and rock back and forth as I could hear someone running. Suddenly, the bus doors flew open, Brent jumped out and threw his arms around me and gave me a hug. Wow! I couldn't believe it. It had only been a year since I last saw him with Dreve, but Brent looked very different. He looked very healthy and seemed happy to see me and be back home in Knoxville (Brent is from Knoxville like myself). Brent had gained a lot of weight, mostly muscle, and now had many tattoos on his arms. I remembered him as a short, shinny little white guy with a great big heart. People close to Brent told me that Atlantic, and others in the industry, had spent considerable sums of money, just on helping to develop Brent's new image. I can't verify the accuracy of that statement, but I know that Brent has always seemed genuine to me.

Smith greeted me with a big grin and the words "Hey brother! How ya been man?" I told him I was great and was at UT working on my master's degree and writing for the university newspaper *The Daily Beacon*. I teased him and asked "Man, what have they got you on, growth hormone? Look at you! Long hair and tattoos!" He laughed and invited me up into his bus to meet the rest of Shinedown.

Being the ever gracious host, Brent must have bragged about me to his bandmates, because I sat down facing the band's guitarist Jasin Todd (At that time. Jasin later left Shinedown), who said to me "Hey man, I'm Jasin. Brent tells us you're an incredible writer. He said you're the best in Knoxville." I thanked him, shook his hand, and introduced myself to everyone. I was probably blushing at that point. Shinedown were so friendly when I met them, and were excited to finally play in Knoxville. They made me and everyone on the bus feel welcome.

I got a hold of some demo CDs of Shinedown that were being given away at that show. While on the bus, I shared with them how I had interviewed famed, Grammy-winning, rapper Sir Mix A Lot. I explained to them that Mix loved heavy metal and hard rock, and at the time was producing some metal bands. I had all the members of Shinedown sign the demo CD, and I mailed it to Sir Mix A Lot along with the first CD of a great band from Knoxville called 10 Years, who a short while later got signed by Universal Records. Now both bands have obtained fortune and fame... The world can thank me for promoting them later... *grin*

After spending some time catching up on current events with Shinedown, I was blown away at the energy and musicianship Brent had developed with them. It became clear and obvious that Brent Smith indeed had a lot of horse sense, but managed to not compromise his values and become part of a self-absorbed herd. I watched and listened to the band perform on a stage accented by black Shinedown tapestry and strobe lights. The band complimented the show's ambiance by all of its members wearing black shirts and pants in a packed club with the lights turned off, except for a few on the stage. After the show ended, I spoke with the band for about fifteen minutes. They were all drenched in sweat and looked exhausted. It was quite a scene as the band walked off the stage. Crews of technicians and club employees scrambled to get the band's gear taken down and loaded into a cargo trailer hitched to the bus.

Careful not to disappoint any fans, the obviously tired members of Shinedown were still able to pause in the early morning hours to sign autographs and have themselves photographed with fans. Brent apologized for not being able to chat long, and attributed his brevity to being in a hurry to meet with his family and some close friends. I told him not to worry about it. After all, it was about 2:00am and I wanted him to see his family and get some rest. Brent and the fellas shared with me that they would be back in Knoxville soon to play at the Civic Coliseum with Three Doors Down, Seether, and Our Lady Peace. Naturally, I made plans to attend.

I remember the first thing I did when I confirmed that Shinedown was indeed scheduled to play at the Knoxville Civic Coliseum, was I called the local promotion and booking agency AC Entertainment. After phoning and speaking with AC Entertainment's Amanda Tullos, she instructed me to contact Shinedown's representatives at McGathy Promotions in New York. This process involved utilizing the etiquette I mentioned earlier in this chapter. At the time of the call, I was ready and prepared with a pen and legal-pad of paper on hand. Of course, I introduced myself with a suave, confident heir of professional sophistication along with a clear voice and concise rhetoric in order to cut-to-the-chase and not waste time. I have found in my years of experience scheduling interviews and coordinating events, that most professionals in the entertainment industry stay busy with their jobs and demand efficient use of their time.

Ms. Tullos told me to call McGathy and make arrangements to do an interview with Shinedown. As instructed, I phoned and spoke with Gwyther Bultman at In De Goot Entertainment. He had a very cordial and professional phone voice, sounding much like a radio DJ. Mr. Bultman seemed pleased and supported my idea to interview Shinedown for the Knoxville Journal. Gwyther's exercise of professional etiquette was obvious when we spoke. Like my paternal grandmother use to tell me: "you catch a lot more flies with honey than vinegar."

After checking with Brent Smith and Shinedown, Mr. Bultman emailed me and let me know that my uncle, David Hester, and I were both approved to be on the guest list. Concert day would prove to be a big dose of "horse sense" for me as I recall. That day began rather roughly. I awoke with a bloated, cramping stomach and diarrhea. Lovely... I had just spent the two previous days out of work, because I had some sort of nasty virus that plagued me with headaches, fevers, dry mouth, vomiting, and just generally feeling crummy. Therefore, I was taking a strong antibiotic known as a "Z Pack," and Valtrex, that medication you get for herpes. No, I didn't have crabs... Fever blisters and cold sores are forms of herpes kids.

Anyhow, I was feeling and looking pretty rough to begin that day. I remember my prayers to the Almighty as I muttered "Oh, please God… Not today… This isn't happening… Please, Lord you KNOW how much this means to me… Please, heal me and let me go to this concert. Help me write a great article Lord." After having saltine crackers and Sprite for breakfast, I felt better. This was a big day for me, and for Shinedown, and no one or no thing was going to screw it up! Period. So much to do… So little time… As you might imagine, I wasn't feeling particularly spectacular on the two prior days, so laundry hadn't been done.

There were no groceries in tha house! No film for the camera! No gas in my gas-guzzling, high-octane-running, BMW! I gotta call Mike (friend at the Knoxville Journal)! I gotta call Roy (Shinedown's manager at that time)!, I gotta call David! My uncle lives in the sticks and will take two hours to get here! AAARRRGGG!!! Why?!?!? "Okay, just calm down James. Remember Wayne's World… Think happy, think positive… Play some Nappy Roots… That's it…That's it… 'All life, I been po', but it really don't matter anymo'… And they wonder why we act this way…Everything's gonna be okay…"

At around noon that day, I phoned Shinedown's manager. All kinds of noise was in the background from technicians in the middle of sound-checks. He sounded busy, as I could tell he was walking around with his cell phone, plus talking periodically to others while we were conversing. He told me to "Hold on a minute." I waited patiently as I could hear Roy telling roadies where and how stuff was to be setup. About five minutes later (seemed longer on the phone, as I was excited and anxiously trying to score the interview), Roy comes back and says to me "Can you be here an hour before the show? We'll do the interview then. It'll have to be quick, like fifteen minutes, because Brent and the guys have to meet and hangout with their friends and families, plus contest winners." With an adulating smile on my face, I told him "No, problem. We'll be there!" He finished the call telling me to leave my cell phone on, just in case, and so we could find each other.

My uncle was the photographer for that event, plus he knew guitarist Hector Rodriguez of Brent Smith's previous band Dreve. We were on the guest list, but did not know until we arrived at the coliseum, and told security who we were, that free tickets for each of us would be waiting! I had already bought three tickets to cover myself, and my uncle and his girlfriend. No one ever said along the way that we would receive tickets also. I just knew we could go backstage to interview Shinedown. I got an education that night about entertainment etiquette and preparing for interviews. I made it a personal rule after that to always check and make for certain whether or not I, and whoever would be with me, could get into a show for free.

Generally, I have found as a media writer that entertainers, or just whomever I will write about or interview will, as a courtesy, give me free tickets and access to whatever I am writing about. Of course, I have to present myself professionally, and provide some background and contact info, but usually most folks I have written about are cordial and agreeable. Perhaps, folks just can't say no to my warm charisma, charming good looks, pleasant demeanor, and impeccable reputation for my written work. *grin* Or actually, as Annie Lennox sang in the Eurythmics hit *Sweet Dreams*, "Some of them want to use you…Some of them want to get used by you." Entertainers usually won't turn down any good free promotions or publicity. Heck, it doesn't necessarily have to be good either. Sometimes, controversy over things some folks find offensive, can actually help promotion and sales.

Such would seem to have been the case for the rap and hip-hop group *2 Live Crew*. In 1989, the group released it's controversial third album "As Nasty As They Want to Be." It contained the popular single *Me So Horny*. In June of 1990, a Broward County, Florida judge ruled that the group's third release was legally obscene. After an appeal, that ruling was overturned based on the First Amendment right to freedom of speech. I remember that year in high school, as the controversy incited teens everywhere to run out and purchase, or bootleg, copies of the material. The said album, went on to sell three million copies.

In 1990, the group's frontman Luther Campbell, and the crew, released the album "Banned in the USA," which featured a song of the same title and parodied the hit song "Born In The USA" by rocker *Bruce Springsteen*. On the same record, was the song *Mamolapenga*, which many in the Latin-American community found to be controversial or offensive. That same year in September, the group's label "Luke Skyywalker Records" paid director George Lucas a $300,000 settlement out of court for Campbell using the popular *Star Wars* character's name as his stage name. In 1991, Luther Campbell was court-ordered to pay artist *MC Shy D* $1.6 million dollars, after a dispute over royalties. In 1994, the U.S. Supreme Court ruled that 2 Live Crew's parody of Roy Orbison's hit song *Pretty Woman* was not plagiarism, under the Fair Use Doctrine. In June 1995, the group's frontman Luther Campbell filed for bankruptcy. Mr. Campbell and his companions obviously experienced some of the tougher aspects of being celebrity musicians.

Given the mixed reactions of fans and the public media, I am sure that Campbell and 2 Live Crew learned a lot about technicalities of the entertainment business such as marketing, copyright laws, liabilities, and demographics. One can note that the more controversial and popular their music was, then the more it sold. Rapper *Sir Mix A Lot* told me in an interview that he started not to release his anthem "Baby Got Back," due to the questionable nature of its lyrics, which some labeled as both racist and sexist material. The artist shared that his good friend rapper Chuck D of the legends *Public Enemy* encouraged him to release the song.

Mr. Ridenhour (Chuck D) was no stranger to argument over his thought- provoking music. Having formally earned a bachelor degree in Graphic Design, but perhaps a PhD in streetwise knowledge, Mr. Chuck did not shy away from discussing sensitive issues such as racism, inequality, politics, and corrupt law enforcement. Perhaps the name of the group summed up the essence of its music on songs like *911 Is a Joke*, a tune which some in the media frenzied to expose, while others demanded it be censored and asked for an apology from those artists. It expressed dissatisfaction among members of the African-American community, and other minorities, over how the 911 emergency system allegedly failed to provide the same qualities, levels, and availability of its services to racial minorities as it did to White people.

As I said in the beginning of this chapter, being a rock star isn't always good, and it isn't always easy. Brent Smith and Shinedown concurred as the band shared in its interview that they felt an added sense of responsibility to perform well and to please family, friends, and fans whenever they have performed in their hometowns.

When I first interviewed Shinedown in 2003, all of the band agreed that playing its hometowns was usually more stressful than performing in others, because they were in a place where a lot of people personally knew them. Brent Smith told me "You would think that it would be easier playing in your hometown, because you're used to it, but it's not. It's actually easier for us to play places where people don't know us. If you screw up in a show, that sucks, but you don't have to answer to people you personally know who are disappointed in you. We don't want to disappoint anyone, but it's a lot harder when friends and family are mad at you."

There were many great bands, musicians, and people working in the industry in those hometowns who didn't have the fortune of getting signed to a major record label like the members of Shinedown. All of Shinedown's members voiced genuine appreciation and respect for that. I guess Brent and Shinedown have gained a lot of horse sense by now. I would estimate that the number of shows that each member of

Shinedown has performed in would be in the thousands, both together, and before Shinedown. I am sure that traveling together everyday for years, and spending countless hours together has helped them develop some wisdom along the way.

Perhaps, another example of some entertainers gaining wisdom in the course of their work is the song "Roses" by the Atlanta hip-hop supergroup *Outkast*. I heard the reason for the song's zany lyrics was because the group learned they could sing, write, or say pretty much whatever they wanted to, and if they made it sound good, it didn't matter what the topic was, because people would still buy it. Interestingly, the song's character "Caroline" is a prostitute (which are common in Atlanta and other big cities) trying to market or sell herself. Outkast had amassed such strong support from its fans, and was so charismatic and likable, that their singing "roses tend to smell like pooh-pooh" did not diminish the group's sales. Rather, it was a catalyst for more.

Enough about everyone else's wisdom! Folks want to know how I gained more knowledge and wisdom in the industry, right? Well, I'm gonna break it down for ya. Here are some tips on how to live what the artist *Prince* referred to as "the glamorous life:"

1. Believe in yourself. People won't buy what your selling, if you don't buy it first. Don't be an arrogant prick, but be confident.

2. It's doesn't matter if you think what you did sucks, as long as fans still like it and support you. I know that sounds like corporate greed, but it's true. So, don't be afraid to make a mess. There have been plenty of times when I played music in front of people, and I hit sour notes, but I just smiled real big, took a look around to see if folks were going to lynch me, and when they didn't, I just smiled some more, danced around like an idiot, and made people laugh. Just play it off.

3. Don't interrupt people in the middle of their pleasure. If the crowd is entertained, then you've earned your money. Don't stop a good thing. It doesn't matter if you walk out on stage and puke all over the crowd. If they like it, then bring out "Ralph!"

4. Work with people you know and trust. It can take some time to get to know folks, but it's worth it. I have learned that there are plenty of great artists and entertainers, who have wonderful ideas, but you can't always trust them or depend on them. I have been let down plenty of times by folks who for whatever reason, weren't able to deliver on their words. Don't take it personally and don't give up on your dream. You might have to stop listening to people

you can't rely on, but don't be quick to judge them or write them off completely. Things happen. Life happens. This book wasn't finished when I said it would be. I shouldn't have told so many people about it before it was finished, but I learned an important lesson. I learned to keep my big mouth SHUT.

5. Make no mistakes, only changes. Don't be afraid of the unknown!

6. Remember the old proverb that "what doesn't kill you can only make

7. you stronger." You can be your own best friend or choose to be your own enemy. Be like Chumbawamba. If you get knocked down, then get right back up again.

In my many years of attending shows, I have seen, heard, and experienced much. From my experiences, I have gained a lot of wisdom and I have learned that anything can happen. I recall being a guest for a show one evening that ultimately earned me a warehouse full of "browny points." I was covering indy, cult-favorite, jazz greats *Sun Ra Arkestra*. Anyhow, I was hanging out backstage with these cats, you know, just mingling. Our discussion mainly centered around the preview article I wrote for a newspaper and how it turned out, but two great things happened at this show: I learned an important lesson from the band and I saved the club and Sun Ra Arkestra potentially thousands of dollars.

First of all, while we were hanging out backstage I was reminded of something I have come to notice about many popular musicians. While I was chatting with some horn players, one of them said to me "Hey man, I like your shoes. Where did you get those sneakers? What kind are they?" This reminded me that artists often don't really want to talk about their works, rather they just want to hangout and talk, like average, everyday people. They don't want to be treated differently. Sure, they want respect and good service from people they work with, but I've noticed most are turned off by crazed fans who run toward them all wild-eyed and talking loudly. It also looks bad if you're supposed to be doing professional work, but you're acting like an amateur. When I'm with a celebrity or a famous person, I don't see that person as being above me in status. I am just as good enough and as interesting as any rock star I've met. I might have a better personality than some folks I've met, but I'm not better than anyone, and no one is better than me.

You might be wondering how I saved the band and the club some money. It's quite easy actually. When your name is James Hester, you've got "connections." *grin* We were conversing, of course, and the guitarist of the group nervously asked me "Hey man, you wouldn't happened to know anyone close by who has a guitar amp do you?" I asked why and he proceeded to tell me about how somebody had poured something all over his amplifier. He needed an amp ASAP, because the opening band had just finished playing. So, I reply "Ah man, that sucks! Hold on a minute. Let me think... I have an uncle with a business a few blocks from here and his son keeps his band's equipment stored there. Let me try calling him."

I pulled out my cell phone and went through my wallet. I found my uncle Scott's card, but it had his home phone handwritten on it too. I called and asked to speak with my cousin James Brady, an incredible aspiring artist himself. James was mellow as usual (must run in the family) and he asked me what's up. I explained things to him while I stood proudly in front of Sun Ra Arkestra's guitarist. James, of course, was cool and agreed to help. He told me he had a Marshall 4x12 cabinet and also a Mesa Boogie 4x12 cabinet. I told the bewildered axeman (sorry I forget his name) "Alright, we've got two amps for you to choose from. All you have to do in return is let my cousin into the show for free." "Fine! I really appreciate it. We'll clear it with the club's manager," he said.

We went to the manager and explained what happened. The club's manager (of course the name of the manager and club are not mentioned so as to save any embarrassment) gasped "Wow! Oh my God! James (me), you are on the guest list PERMANENTLY. No questions asked. Thank you so much for your help!" My cousin told me that I had to come pick up the amp and get him, because he didn't have a ride that night. I went and got James and the amp, then returned to the venue, all in fifteen minutes. Thus, special agent Hester saved the show and all involved with only a momentary delay!

I am reminded of another high-profile event where I gained a good measure of horse sense. I was a guest for the rock band *Three Doors Down*. After dining on the fine catered cuisine backstage and chatting with some radio jocks, members of Three Doors Down were hanging out and being sociable. Understandably, they were very popular and very busy. I chatted briefly with the group's lead vocalist Brad Arnold for an article I was working on. Well, after we spoke I asked "Hey, can I get a photo of us together?" He said "Yeah, sure. Let me clear it with my publicist." I spoke with the publicist. I showed him my camera and my pass, but that didn't matter.

He insisted that a photographer traveling with the band take the photo. He explained that the photo would be printed out backstage while I waited, so naturally I agreed. Well, a mob of groupies overheard me talking to Brad and they rushed over gleefully wanting to be in the photo with us. Not ones to disappoint the ladies, Brad and I agreed to a nice group photo. Well, I had other folks at the venue that I had to write about and talk with that night, so after waiting fifteen minutes I split with the hope of returning to get my prize photo at a later time. You guessed it. I returned and to learn that the groupies had taken all of the photos. No sweat.

I just called Three Door's publicist the next day and explained. Whoever it was I spoke with at the time said she would email me the photo. Perhaps, she did and it landed in my spam-filled bulk mail, or maybe it just never got sent. I have no hard feelings toward Three Doors Down or any of the band's associates. It's really no one's fault. It's not a big deal. THINGS HAPPEN. However, I did learn that the musicians often have someone take photos for them, so they can retain the copyrights to those photos. I learned after that to always get approval for photography, and get a photographer, before I meet with celebrities.

Lastly, don't be afraid to be an "easy rider." Practically every professional entertainer I know or have met travels frequently. Get used to this. So many of them are contracted to perform in hundreds, or even thousands, of places year-round, so commonly they use tour buses, limos, and airplanes. Learn to accept that life as a "rock star," can indeed be lonely at times. One day you might wake up in the cramped bed of your tour bus asking yourself "What town am I in? What day is this? And where are my clothes?" Take a moment to wipe the crust from your eyes, brush yourself off, sip some caffeine, and remember you're the one who asked for all of this, so don't complain. Complaining isn't good PR, and it tends to make you less marketable. If you're out on the trail one day and you fall off the horse with good sense, just get back on and keep riding it until you're the smarter one.

CHAPTER TWO

It Ain't All Glitz n' Glamor

Being rich or famous isn't always swell. There are plenty of entertainers who hate their lives, or at least sometimes wish they were better. Such would seem to have been the case for late actress, model, and reality TV icon Vicki Marshall, who was better known as Anna Nicole Smith. As if her own fortune and fame were not enough, the platinum-blonde-haired bombshell was also skillful enough as an "exotic dancer" to catch the eyes and garner the affections of late billionaire oil tycoon J. Howard Marshall. The two eventually agreed to a highly publicized and controversial marriage, which held regard by some as nothing more than a gold-digging attempt by Smith to relieve Marshall of at least some of his fortune.

After all, the successful oil king was old enough to be Anna's father and her professional work did not receive as much esteem from others as it did from Marshall. In spite of peculiar circumstances surrounding their relationship, Anna Nicole insisted in interviews aired on television that she and Howard had genuine love for one another. So, in a nutshell, she was a beautiful, charismatic, woman with immense fortune and fame. However, given her background and career choices, some found it odd that a poor stripper and porn star would become married to a successful oil baron.

Perhaps, another reason why Smith had commanded the attention and admiration of millions of fans, was her real-life fairy tale of how she had gone from the rags and challenges of a poor girl, who married and became pregnant at a young age, to having become a wealthy inspiration for millions as a spokesperson for the dietary aid *TrimSpa*. Smith gained amounts of weight which greatly altered the physical appearance of the body she was famous for sharing on the pages of *Playboy*. However, after she successfully lost weight with the assistance of TrimSpa, she became a model and spokesperson for the product. Many unusual, some might say bizarre, circumstances often surrounded the late Anna Nicole's life. In spite of her successful career as a nude model, actress for adult films, and hosting her very own TV show, the diva shared with numerous sources prior to her tragic death that she was "lonely and sad."

Smith's childhood and adolescence are reported in the media to have been both unstable and tumultuous. Allegations of her having been a victim of physical, sexual, and mental abuse during her childhood have surfaced. To further complicate her life and distress Anna Nicole, her son Daniel Smith was found dead of an apparent prescription drug-related death September 10, 2006. An already pregnant Smith bore the brunt of emotional scars as she is reported to have been very close to her son Daniel. He was only 20 years old when he died. Ironically, is that also having surfaced is evidence of Anna Nicole's alleged substance abuse or misuse of prescribed medications which, according to some reports, were linked to her death.

If, indeed, abuse was present in Anna Nicole's life, the reports of her numerous short-lived intimate affairs and romances may have been a result of her emotional state which stemmed from the said abuse. At any rate, reports regarding Smith's life suggest that it was not as glamorous and fantastic as the entertainment industry had often portrayed it. Her highly publicized, and questionable, relationship with her attorney Howard K. Stern alluded to some of the eccentricities of her lifestyle.

A controversial video of Smith, recorded by Stern prior to her death, aired on numerous television news programs. The video, free of any glitz and glamour one might come to expect from Anna Nicole, shows her disheveled face painted with clown makeup as she struggles to articulate simple words and phrases during the clip. It suggests Smith might have been intoxicated during that moment. After having watched the video, I was saddened that television media, and other sources, aired its content. Just because a person is already famous does not give anyone the right to exploit that person's mishaps. Many would argue the public has a right to know the truth, but it is a biased belief of this writer that sometimes discretion "is the better part of valor," and is often a reflection of one's integrity.

Philip Anselmo, who has been a major influence for my work ethic and determined spirit, spoke candidly in interviews about how not-so-great the life of being a rock star can be. At the height of his career, he was interviewed, along with Dimebag Darrell of Pantera, for *Hard 'N Heavy* rock video magazine. Mr. Anselmo shared about how he was unfairly harassed, scrutinized, and disrespected simply for the way he looked and for his employment with Pantera. During that interview (1991), his head was shaved bald. Because NAZI skinheads and racism were popular during that time, he was unduly profiled by "cops" and stereotyped for the way he appeared. Also in that interview, Anselmo described some of the burden of being responsible for the security and control of crowds at his performances. Pantera shows were noted for being loud, and full of angry adolescents in raging mosh pits.

In a 2006 interview with TV network VH-1, the vocalist explained some of why he eventually left Pantera. Due to feeling pressured to perform well and honor his contracts with the music industry, Philip turned to heroin, alcohol, and other drugs to try and mask the agonizing pain he felt in his back as a result of past injuries and the condition of his spine. After seeing the VH-1 interview, the personal experience I had at one of Philip's shows a few years ago made more sense. First of all, I just want to say that Philip Anselmo had an incredible voice and his singing and vocals on Pantera's *Vulgar Display of Power* were artwork. However, when I saw him perform with Hank Williams, III and the metal band *Superjoint Ritual*, Mr. Anselmo's vocals were reduced to noisy grunts and screams, because he was a sloppy, drunk, intoxicated, mess.

Anselmo stumbled around onstage with a teetering microphone and a nasty disposition. I believe the veteran performer must have realized in some way that he risked having a crowd of angry fans, so he played his "wild card," and saved the show. He stopped and made an offer that some of us lunatic fans could not refuse. He said "Our stage is your stage. Make some noise! Get up here on this stage and jump! I want you to go completely insane!" At that moment, I was hanging out with shadowWax's lead singer Eric Christopher and Copper drummer (during that time) Eric Yarber. We looked at each other and we were like: "I don't know man... We're adults. What if we get hurt? We couldn't work or play any shows."

Something deep inside of me just snapped. Must have been the testosterone, because I was completely sober. Ever since I was in high skull and first heard Pantera, I had dreamed of stage diving at one of their shows, but they broke up and I never got that opportunity. This was it. It was as close to my dream as I could make it. I told Christopher and Yarber "Life is short. Watch this!" I made my way through the crowd, up front to the stage, and the club bouncers at Blue Cats knew me, so they let me get on stage. It was like a dream for about 30 seconds.

I walked out between Philip Anselmo and Hank Williams III, threw my rock horns in the air, pointed to some guys in the crowd, ran, and jumped in! Splat! I landed on top of the hands of the many as they slung me around like a ragdoll, quickly surfing my way across the room and onto the floor. THANK YOU GOD! I didn't end up in the hospital, but I did get a little banged up and sore. It was all surreal standing on the stage beside one of my favorite musicians (Philip) from my high skull days. The rational side of me was a little scared, as the stage lights did not penetrate the darkness of the club very far from the stage. "Now or never James... The crowd is waiting," I thought to myself. I was so high on adrenaline that I didn't even feel the pain in my feet until the next morning.

I learned a very important lesson at Philip and Hank's show: NEVER STAGE-DIVE WEARING CONVERSE CHUCK TAYLOR SNEAKERS. All I wore during that dive was a t-shirt, shorts, and those high-top Chucks. What I did was stupid. The morning after the show, the toes on both of my feet were purple and my feet were blue and swollen. I don't think I had any broken bones, but I should never have done that. I was 27 years old and working full-time on my master's degree at the University of Tennessee. The limelight and the stage-diving antics really were not necessary. I could have been seriously injured, or worse, have hurt someone else. I'm not saying that people shouldn't stage-dive, but I am saying that people should exercise prudent, sober, judgment, and stage-dive carefully.

After the previously mentioned event, while the rest of the band hung out in the club's courtyard chatting with me and discussing how much they enjoyed playing, Philip Anselmo had passed out cold in his tour bus. At the time, I was more disappointed and did not understand the pain Anselmo had endured, but now I know why and I just hope he stays sober and healthy. There are countless other examples of my having been around wasted rock stars, but I chose to write about this one simply because Mr. Anselmo openly explained himself and discussed his behavior on VH-1 Television. Many folks can't begin to imagine the pressures and responsibilities of being an entertainer or a celebrity. Obviously, Philip Anselmo was experiencing both physical as well as emotional pain. I wouldn't wish such torment on anyone. Hopefully, someday Philip Anselmo and I can meet and I can tell him face to face that I respect him and wish him the best.

I recall another less than glamorous evening forever written in the pages of rock history. I went to see a band called Powerman 5000. I remember receiving an email about the event and considering whether or not I should attend. The band's lead vocalist, Spider, is the brother of famed shock artist Rob Zombie. At that time, I knew nothing about Powerman 5000 other than Spider being Rob Zombie's brother, and that I loved White Zombie (Rob's band from my high skull days). I also knew that my buds Brent Smith and Shinedown had just finished a tour with them. Therefore, I figured the show would be at least pretty good.

I can't even remember who the opening artists were that night. I just remember arriving and talking with the club's bouncer Chris, who told me that he didn't know if there would even be a show, because Spider was busy puking his guts up during the sound check. So, I was like "Aw... That sucks! I'm gonna hang out and have a good time anyway!" To my pleasant surprise, the band decided the show must go on, and that they must go on. A blond-haired guy, who looked sorta like Billy Idol during his Generation X years, walked out on stage front and center. Since I didn't have any of the band's CDs, it was a fresh introduction for me. Amid the strobe lights and a dimly lit room, I relaxed and gave the band my attention. Wow! It was very different from White Zombie, but it rocked!

The bouncer Chris told me that the band phoned a doctor about an hour before the show and pumped Spider full of meds. He said when Spider was asked if he wanted to cancel the show, the generous performer stated "Man, I can't quit. Just look at 'em. Look at all those fans lined up to hear us, we can't quit now!" So, Spider took the meds and forged on. Rock on brother. I respect your integrity and your work ethic. Most folks never knew, as I did, that Spider was so ill, but in spite of his sickness, he put on an excellent performance. He was a true performer.

After that show, I hung out with Powerman 5000's drummer Adrian Ost. While drinks were on the house for VIPs, and the club was empty of patrons, we chatted as he cooled down from his performance. He told me that he had "not been with the band long," but added "We really wanted to play here (Blue Cats) tonight, and I don't think Spider would have wanted to let down his fans by not playing this evening, especially after so many people showed up early and waited in long lines for a soldout show." Adrian was a funny guy with a witty, sarcastic demeanor when we met. He had on a t-shirt for CBS' *Late, Late Show with Craig Kilborn*. When I asked him about it he replied "Yeah, we were on there a few nights ago, and all I got was this crummy shirt. Naw...Just kidding." We discussed how great Craig was about supporting musical guests on his show –how so many had played on his program. Before we departed for the evening we had our bartender Ms. Kirsten (also Miss Hawaiian Tropic) snap some "power photos" of Adrian and I.

Anyhow, let's return more directly to recollections of less than glamorous events that happened to this author. There were countless examples of those not-so-fresh experiences in my life, but I'll spare readers of too much drama in this writing. To do this we'll return to my childhood and work our way back to the present ("I'm a big kid now"). I made my first big break in the fourth grade when I sang a solo in some silly little children's play about parts of speech. I remember it well... I was in front of the whole school (or at least a bunch of other kids and teachers) when I shook like a leaf and nervously sang my lines, when it came time for me to. I think the play was called "The Missing Parts of Speech." It wasn't exactly a runaway sensation on Broadway, but hey, one has to start somewhere…

I remember doing rehearsals for that little event. I had to practice singing my lines. I had prepositions. "Around, across, among, to… Against, along, beyond, through… Before, beside, on, under, without… After, during, for, about… These are prepositions, I use them everyday…" Anyhow, I was really hard on myself then and so ambitious. I wanted my solo to be perfect. I wanted to be cool in front of the other kids. So this was HUGE for me. Jamie (as I was called in childhood) was making his debut! Well, I remember freezing up at first onstage, but when it came time to sing my part, I shook like jello on meth. I stuttered a little at first, but then my confidence rose as the volume of my voice crescendoed and I wailed. I may not have sang well, but I could wail.

How do I know? Some archiving, enthused parent (or maybe conniving) videotaped it and my classmates and I watched the aftermath in the school library soon afterward. I would love to get ahold of that piece of evidence… I watched myself on video, me with my head back proudly as I threw my arm up and hand in the air bellowing to the masses. The kids laughed and a school bully started to make fun (I beat him until he cried when we got to junior high) of me, as I was so embarrassed and felt so stupid. But I remember a little girl, I was friends and neighbors with, named Jennifer Hoadley came to my defense telling me "It's okay Jamie, it really wasn't that bad. You did fine. Don't worry about those stupid people."

My best bud Rob Collins was there for me too. Yeah… Screw 'em… I learned my parts of speech so well that I went on to write this book! *grin* Rob was the nerd's nerd, but he was the coolest kid I ever knew. He had a genius mind, earned straight A's, wore glasses, was in all the "gifted" accelerated student classes, was pale, skinny, and allergic to EVERYTHING. Yeah, I was a pale, scrawny little nerd too, but we had strength in numbers. *grin* Rob and I used to hang out a lot and we were in the same Cub Scout Pack, number 451. Of course we went camping together and did things that young nerds like to do such as build fires, study things under microscopes, discover the joys of basic chemistry, and make fun of stupid people. Rob's sarcastic wit was the best. We obviously grew up to become the ambassadors of coolness. Anyhow, the "revenge of the nerds" would follow the next year.

The Fifth Grade… I remember it well. We were famous then. It was the last crummy year of school I would have to spend as a student at Pleasant Ridge Elementary. Ms. Margerie Spears was mine and Rob's teacher. My little-league baseball team *The Mets* won the league championship. That year was my second one playing trumpet. I began playing the previous year in Ms. Able's school band class. That was when my grandmother gave me the sweet King trumpet she got when she was a girl in 1934. I still have that b-flat Liberty Model, and I still play it... Oh yeah, as I was saying REVENGE followed, or at least a little bit of success and coolness. There was a talent show at school that year, and Rob and I played a duet of the song *Big Rock Candy Mountain*. I mean, what could rock harder than that?

Rob was young Benny Goodman on clarinet and I was young Doc Severinsen on trumpet. Ok, it was simply a little ditty for kids that was low-key. But, we played that song. Looking back on it, I'm sure we nailed all of the notes, but I imagine that it sounded a bit robotic, or at least the stage presence was, because we were just kids. I mean we didn't really have that song inside of us. At that time, I lacked the rock and roll spirit I'm now known for. I just didn't have it in my soul then! The wiser I have become, the more I am able to put aside reservations and perform in front of people, no matter how large or small the crowd. Hey, if you're going to screw up, then screw up big! Fifth grade was about the time when I started playing bugle calls for the Scouts. I remember when Cubmaster Harry Carroll first asked me to play. It was for a flag lowering at Pleasant Ridge Elementary School, just before the beginning of a pack meeting in the school cafeteria.

Harry was an Army veteran who met his wife Bridgette, our Den Mother, while stationed in Germany. He thought it was cool to have a kid around that he could teach the bugle calls to. Since I did not know how to play *To the Colors*, I played *Taps* instead. I remember shaking nervously for that too, but Harry encouraged me after nailing *Taps*, by telling me "See there. You played it perfect. Good job Mr. Hester." I never forgot that. Just a little bit of encouragement is all I needed and a little more practice. Harry won't know until after he reads this, just how huge an impact he made on my life with his simple words of encouragement and support. The following year, I went on to become the Bugler in Boy Scouts and Harry became an Assistant Scoutmaster in Troop 448.

Moving forward to 1989, I had the honor of representing East Tennessee at the National Boy Scout Jamboree as the Bugler. I was seen and heard by thousands when I blared bugle calls on my trumpet. By that time, I had developed quite an ego, so I felt particularly cool to be "tooting my own horn" for the masses. August of 1989 was the same summer when I started high skull at Central. Immediately after I returned from the jamboree, I started high skull band camp...Joy... It was upon my mother's urging that I tried to be in the marching band, or so I remember. I remember how awkward I felt trying to learn how to march, especially since I arrived late after band camp had already started. There were some cute girls, of course, who were a little older and tried to help me learn to march, but I just wasn't coordinated at that time to march.

Again, as with my playing *Big Rock Candy Mountain* for that talent show, I wasn't feeling it in my soul. I lacked the rhythm in my boo-tay then. One of the trumpet players was a sweet older girl who tried to help me, but she noticed I was mechanically challenged and once commented "You march like you gotta corn cob stuck up your butt. Loosen up. Relax!" That was just it. I wasn't relaxed then. I was an emotional walking mess of hormones. I was SO screwed up.

To make matters worse on a kid with an inferiority complex, I had a band director who had an ego the size of Alaska with the coldness to go along with. I won't mention his name. The man knew music incredibly well and could direct, but warm and friendly were not his traits. I watched him literally scream at kids and call them names! However, I wasn't too warm and friendly myself. Perhaps, the real problem was that we were BOTH depressed and we simply clashed. I have no hard feelings though. I mean, I wasn't the only kid in school who hated him. *smirk* So, our mutual hatred (plus my lack of ambition and my depression) for one another led to my dropping out of band after my first freshman year at Central.

Yeah, screw him! I said to myself. I'll show them (or so I thought). So, I did what any rebellious zit-faced teen would do, NOTHING... Absolutely NOTHING. I quickly spiraled downward after failing my freshmen year and I started listening to heavier music. The heavier music wasn't bad, but my attitude and how I reacted to that music was. I fell in love with two songs. "Dyers Eve" by *Metallica* resonated with me strongly. James Hetfield growled "Dear mother! Dear father! What is this hell you have put me through?!" Then I discovered the band *Suicidal Tendencies* one day while I was vegging-out in front of the "magic box" watching the *Jukebox Network*. Like a lot of kids, I was mesmerized by music videos, but I was pleasantly blown away one afternoon when the heaviest and most menacing band a miserable kid could love, *Suicidal Tendencies*, splashed across my TV screen. Some crazy Latino dude (Mike Muir the singer and mainstay of the band) in a Kings hockey jersey getting fried in an electric chair and screaming "YOU CAN'T BRING ME DOWN! YOU CAN'T BRING ME DOWN!"

It was fabulous! Especially because racism was SO prevalent at that time and the band's guitarist was a Black dude named Rocky George. Other than Jimi Hendrix, I didn't know that a Black guy could rock so hard. I was narrow-minded and ignorant like most teens, so *Suicidal Tendencies* gave me a real education. Further, the band's bass player was Robert Trujillo who is also Latino. He's currently belting out bass lines for *Metallica*. Latinos and a Black guy playing heavy metal music? It went completely against all of the stereotypical norms established at that time. It wasn't until my young-adult college years later in life when I began to listen to music more than seeing color.

As a kid, my head just about exploded when I found out that my favorite guitarist Slash, of *Guns 'n Roses*, was actually half African-American. It totally didn't fit with the lyrics of one song he played called "One in a Million." A lot of controversy followed that song's release, as many thought it was racist and homophobic. I even had someone once tell me that Axle was racist, and that Rose actually borrowed the song from the racist White-power band known as *Skrewdriver*. I don't know about that, but nevertheless the song sparked much debate over its content. It would also seem odd to me that Slash would put up with Axle being racist or homophobic. Further, the band's record label was Geffen. It is widely known that David Geffen is Jewish. So, maybe that person should verify his information directly with the former members of what was called Guns n' Roses. But, need I digress any further?

Not blaming them, but my musical influences didn't always encourage me to live better. I basically ditched school as much as I could get away with and started hiding from the world. I was SO depressed. My poor mother had a hard time with my two younger teenage brothers and myself. She was a divorced, single, lady working full-time and going to college part-time. It had to be hard on her at times. As I mentioned earlier in the beginning of this book, my father did not consistently support us financially. My dad loved my brothers and me, but unfortunately he wasn't around much to support us after our teen years. So, where was I?

Oh yeah! Central High Skull was hell on earth... Nazis, Crypts, and Bloods, Satanists, FCA, Jocks, Preps, Nerds, Rednecks... So many wonderful, trendy cliques, but I didn't fit into any of them... Let's see... The next less than glamorous event to infringe upon my psyche was that I did not move to California after failing my freshmen year. Mom was engaged to marry a guy, and he lived in San Diego. At the time, it was a dream come true. I had failed, but who cared? I was going to move to San Diego where the weather was nice and NOBODY knew me. I had already acted like a big shot and told all of the kids at Central that I was moving to Callie...

I didn't move to California. I was SO embarrassed. I had to go back to school and face all of those people! On top of that, now all of the kids had learned that I failed and got held back. Suddenly, I was the biggest loser in school (or so I thought). Nobody from the previous year wanted to talk to me anymore. They all laughed at me and thought I was a liar. My mom decided she didn't love the guy deeply enough and called off the plans to marry him and move to San Diego. I wanted to curl up in a cave and die! I was such a mess at that point. Things got better though. There were some cute little freshmen girls who started talking to me and I met Patrick Morehead. He soon became my best friend. He and his brother Daniel moved to Knoxville from Baltimore. Patrick skated and had a funky haircut, plus he was totally sarcastic, but he was smart and made good grades still.

He gave me my first skateboard. He was my hero then. It was his old Alien Workshop deck. I put some ancient Tracker trucks on it and he gave me some Sex Cells wheels by A-1 Meats. I began to skate every day. I skated hard and took a lot of frustrations out on my skateboard. Patrick and I skated street. We liked skating on the stairs and handrails at my apartment community. We did some insane tricks! Thank God we never ended up seriously hurt, because we NEVER wore pads or a helmet. We were testosterone-driven numb skulls! We were too cool to worry about safety. We figured we'd be safe when we were dead. Anyhow, we liked a lot of the same stuff. We liked the same bands: Metallica, Danzig, Misfits, Sepultura, Dead Milkmen, Ministry, Anthrax, Suicidal Tendencies.

We liked the same kind of movies. We went together to the theater to see the special showing of *Nightmare on Elm Street*, but it was not the usual in the series. For a limited time only it was shown in theaters in 3D! We loved it! Freddy Kreuger was our all-time slasher hero! I'll never forget seeing demons flying toward me out of the screen, or almost having my eyes poked out by the razors on Freddy's fingers as they shot out of the screen towards my face. It was SO cool. Further, Freddy was the bad guy. He knew it and he didn't care who else did. Oh, did it get any better than that for a depressed, skinny, little White boy? Freddy! Freddy! Freddy! I haven't seen that movie in years, but I remember nothing about it was scary and I laughed so hard at times that I cried. Nothing made me more cheery in those days than a good slasher movie!

Oops! I caught myself. I was digressing again. I suppose that is not so glamorous for an incredible star of my magnitude. Anyhow, I can recall more less than glamorous events that occurred after moving to Oak Ridge with my mother and brothers. Before I moved out of Oak Ridge to go live with my dad's mother, as mentioned earlier in this book, my buds and I (some are not my friends anymore, plus I want to protect the identity of everyone involved) were going to have a TV show. Whew! Who! To be completely fair it was a low-budget show that would have aired on community-supported public access television. We were ripping off the movie *Wayne's World* and the movie *UHF*.

We all really liked the stuff on the TV shows *Saturday Night Live* and *Kids in the Hall*, plus we loved *Weird Al Yankovic* and the stupid *Monty Python* movies like "Quest for the Holy Grail." We found out about the local public access, "free TV" in Oak Ridge from our friends, and in my quest for stardom, I learned that the low- budget studio, responsible for polluting the airways with our gimmicks, just happened to be right next door to the swank efficiency apartments I lived in. Anyhow, I walked over to the old hotel which housed the Public TV and spoke with the Director one day. He told me about how it all worked and requested I sign up for classes first, and then I could have my own show.

I don't remember all of the exact details, but I remember the fee for the TV production classes was ridiculously cheap. It was less than $100 bucks. Wow! My friends and I were SO excited! We were gonna be famous! This was our humble break. We planned on having a TV show that showcased local artists and supported local music and entertainment, because we were so dedicated to contributing to "all of that which does not suck." We were just selfless, modern Renaissance men. *smirk* Then I got involved in that car accident. Welcome to reality James. No more TV show.

It's okay though, because I haven't given up on my dreams. They'll just come about a little later or I'll have new ones. One of my friends, whom I mentioned in the first chapter, Matt Hall, went on with his band *New Brutalism* to record and work with Steve Albini (he produced Nirvana, L7, Big Black and others we admired) and also with Bob Weston (he engineered for Stone Temple Pilots). I've been told that Matt also went on to earn his PhD from *Harvard University* in Architectural Design. For a year or two after that accident it bothered me a little that it wasn't me instead, or me working on music and gigs with Matt.

I'm really proud of Matt and I am in no way jealous of him. He's an incredible guy with a lot of talent and heart. My wonderful wife Katie reminds me often that she married me for who I am and not for my accomplishments or money. She explained to me that awards and material wealth doesn't validate me or make me any better or lesser an individual. The same holds true for Matt and all of my friends and family. They are all more than just names, fame, and fortune.

I am reminded of other less than glamorous events that happened both before and during the writing of this book. The first would be my having met a legendary hard rock band while I was in high skull. While I was a student at Central High, I went to see the monstrous MTV hairspray favorite, *Quiet Riot*. They played a show at what was called *The Electric Ballroom*. It was July 9, 1992 and I remember that day well. Quiet Riot was one of the first bands to appear on MTV and were one of my childhood favorites. The band's platinum-selling classic "Metal Health" kept me sane during my awkward boyhood.

After having seen them on MTV and listening to them on the radio for years, one might think that a huge crowd would come out to a sold-out show for such veteran performers, or at least that's what I thought. Then reality smacked my eyes and ears upon arriving and staying for the event. I didn't stand in line long waiting to get in. While waiting in line, I stole a really cool yellow poster from a wall featuring the band's lead singer Kevin Dubrow wearing a hockey mask and a straight-jacket. I probably have it still to this day.

It was my first time going to that club. I remember entering the dark, dimly-lit, old warehouse made of brick. It was almost empty, except for a few fans grouped together around the stage and some sitting on the floor with their backs against the walls like some sort of homeless zombies. How could it have been? Where were all of the freakin' people? It was *Quiet Riot*! Or was it? I am not knocking the band or the club, because the low patronage might have been because the group did not contain the same lineup that made it a huge success. Who knows? I remember the opening bands that night were *Wallstreet* and *Dancing with Ellie*. One or both of the opening acts was from Nashville. Anyhow, after hearing Wallstreet open up first, I remember the lead singer coming down offstage and I saw him walking around.

I don't remember his name, but he was very cordial and friendly. I asked him "Man, this is crazy. Why the low turnout??? Quiet Riot are great!" He didn't know why, but replied "I don't know where everybody is. Hey! You wanna meet em'?" He grinned real big and I followed him backstage, outside at the tourbuses. He introduced me to a cool vocalist who sang for Dancing with Ellie. Quiet Riot's legendary lead singer Kevin Dubrow (R.I.P.) walked by and I said "Hi." He paused briefly, and while shaking my hand quietly said "Hey man, thanks for coming out." Dubrow kept on walking as it was obvious he was preparing himself for a performance.

Then I looked over and there he was... Adjusting the strap on his Les Paul guitar. He was my hero! It was Quiet Riot's guitarist Carlos Cavazo! Oh my gosh! The shred-god of head banging! It was like being in a dream for me for a few seconds. I chatted some with Carlos, but soon had to go because he was getting ready too. He told me to come back later after the show and talk to him. ROCK n' ROLL!!! "James world! James world! Party time! Excellent!!!" The next band Dancing with Ellie played a really cool and funky set and then Quiet Riot came out. By that time, a small crowd of about 30 had amassed in front of the stage and the venue had a raucous crowd of about 50 headbangers.

I believe the bassist that night was Kenny Hillery. He played well, but I never have learned much about him. The drummer that night was Bobby Rondinelli. He was great and I learned that he has also played drums for Black Sabbath, Rainbow, Blue Oyster Cult, and Scorpions. Currently, he hosts drum clinics and is the co-author of the book "The Encylopedia of Double-Bass Drumming." It's so funny looking back on that evening, because Carlos during the middle of his playing utilized a classic promotional tool by taking some guitar picks and throwing them out to fans.

Some were in a nice, neat, line up and down on his mic stand which was lined with black electrical tape to hold them. However, I was special. In the middle of his playing, Carlos stopped and threw a pick to me! Yeah! Mine was played on. Ooh...Aww... *smirk* I still have that pic saved in a nice little container. Don't misunderstand me. I know it's just a white *Dean Markley* pic without the band's name on it, but to a young, naïve, greasy-faced boy, it had magical powers that could turn me into a shredder and get me chicks! Or something like that...

It was a great show and I really enjoyed it. That night must have caught the band at a bad time, or else it just wasn't promoted well, because the group's classic "Metal Health" reached #1 on the Billboard charts and it sold over six million copies in the U.S. alone. So, instead of playing in front of 50,000 fans, the band played to a thousand times less, but hey, if they enjoyed doing it, then it was worth it, right? Let's move forward to events I experienced while I was in graduate school at the University of Tennessee.

How could I forget the *Moby* concert, and the events which led up to my going to that show? What a sweet memory... First, I found out about the show because I was writing for a local newspaper. Well, the editor of the Entertainment section of the paper and I... well... I guess we clashed.

Okay, I think the real rift might have come from the few times when I stole the spotlight from her on a few articles, and when I sort of "blew smoke in her face" a few times by giving tips on how to meet people and get good story leads.

I mean, I was a graduate student and a little older, so I was just trying to help. Now that I have a little more wisdom and seasoned experience as a writer, I understand how I should have been. Getting to the point... We were given choices on articles and who to meet. I chose to meet guitarist *Jerry Cantrell* (Alice in Chains) and write about his show. She chose to write about Moby and his show, and maybe meet him the week after Jerry's show. Uh...Oh... Ooh-Kay. Here's where things got interesting. First of all, I just want readers to know that I'm not mentioning her name, because I'm not a slanderous prick and I have better character than that. I don't have any hard feelings toward that editor and I wish her all the best.

As I said, things got interesting... Well, I knew the manager and a lot of the employees at Blue Cats where Jerry Cantrell played, plus I had friends at the local radio stations, so I already had the low-down on where and when to meet the guy. I was V.I.P baby! Earlier in the day, before Jerry's show he did a meet n' greet at a really cool music store on Chapman Highway called *The Disc Exchange*. Naturally, my best bud Eric Davis and I went there before the show and got Jerry to sign some stuff, plus had our photo taken with him. Later on that evening, Jerry and his touring band *Comes With the Fall* played an incredible, sold-out, show and Eric and I got to hang out and meet everyone backstage. It is of course no surprise that I wrote both excellent preview and review articles for this memorial. *smirk*

When I met Jerry before the show, I gave him a copy of the paper with my preview, and then I probably sent his reps the review afterwards also. On the other hand... The next week came and folks were preparing for the "big" Moby concert at the Coliseum. It was on the radio being hyped up for days prior. Of course, Eric and I being the real life "Dynamic Duo" heard on the radio about free tickets being given away downtown in Knoxville on Market Square on some day during that week. We got them of course. I was even a helpful fella and emailed that editor to let her know ahead of time that 300 free tickets were to be given away. *Snicker* So, concert night came. The "big" night. My date and I went. We'll call her "Special K." Eric and his girlfriend at the time were there too.

We got there and hardly anyone was there yet, so we went down on the floor in front of the stage, so we could get a good view. Quickly, we found Eric and his girl and sat down near them. About 30 minutes went by and we were on the floor right in front of the stage, with only a small crowd. And then it happened... Dirty Vegas came out on stage to open and the lights went out in the arena! They were cool. I looked around and thought "This is crazy! Where is everybody? It's Moby!" Eric and I couldn't believe it. Eric grew up in Las Vegas and it shocked him that hardly anyone had showed up yet, so we figured that people were just dissing the opening band and more would come later.

Shortly after Dirty Vegas had begun to play, the band performed its hit "Days one By," which was featured on a Mitsubishi commercial. Awesome! I was so glad I was close to them, so I could watch the hands of the performers. Soon, my man Moby hit the stage! Unbelievable. The lights and sound were fantastic! I couldn't believe it. Moby actually played guitar that night. He had picked it up along the way, I supposed. His new album was popular on the radio and Eric said it was "big in Vegas."

In spite of great lighting and sound, it looked as if someone had lost money on this show. He should have been booked to play at a smaller venue. I guess demographics were poor in Knoxville that night. In the parking garage, on my way out, I saw that editor and like a jerk I asked her "Hey! Did ya get to meet Moby?" I think readers can follow me with this story. I'm not trying to slander anyone involved with that Moby concert. It's just one of those events that I learned a lot from. Now I look back on it and laugh. Hopefully, everyone else can too, because rock n' roll has too much heartbreak and life is too short.

Other less than glamorous experiences I have had include meeting various pretty young women prior to my becoming married. Out of respect and love for my wife Katie I rarely discuss such events. Besides, meeting those girls was never as exciting and wonderful as it was when I met my beautiful and lovely wife Katie. Finding deep and meaningful love that supersedes physical attraction is so much better than shallow "puppy love" or lust like the kinds rock stars often encounter. Anyhow, I am particularly reminded of an event I was a guest for (back in my college days) called the Bourbon Bowl Bash. It was a celebration of the big rivalry between the University of Tennessee's football team and the University of Kentucky's football team. I suppose it was named such due to both state's renown fame for producing intoxicating liquors.

I remember the special emcee's for the event were rock radio DJ "Mancow" and his radio program cohorts "Freak and Turd." I forget what bands played that evening (geez, that's not so glamorous) because I don't remember them being that good, but I do remember that the focus of the show seemed more to be on the bourbon than the music. With that said, some girl apparently either had too much to drink or didn't mind the money, because she stumbled across the stage topless and started taking the rest of what little bit of clothing she had off. Ho hum... "What a slut" I thought to myself, but my thoughts quickly changed.

At that time, I was mingling with an attractive young lady and enjoying casual conversation with her. I remember saying to her "Oh my God, can you believe it? Look at her. That's so skanky." I don't remember the attractive girl's name, but we'll call her Candy. Well, Candy put me in my place. She said to me "I'm a dancer and it doesn't mean I'm a slut or a hoe. The money's good and I've got two kids. I dropped out in 10th grade and I can't make that kind of money anywhere else. A lot of girls would rather be doing other work if they could. They're just trying to make it like anyone else. You shouldn't be so judgmental."

"Oh my God. I'm scum," I thought to myself. I felt about an inch tall at that moment. I mean who was I to judge anyone? Candy told me that she was a stripper at a local club. Stumbling on my words from my foot stuck in my mouth, I muttered "I understand and I apologize if I offended you, but I just disagree with that line of work. I don't find what she did to be attractive, rather degrading." I walked off feeling like a complete idiot. I mean who was I? Saint James? Not quite. I've done plenty of controversial things in my life and have fallen short of being respectable on many occasions. So, for me to try and condemn anyone would be complete hypocrisy.

I know that my values and opinions regarding "adult entertainment" might differ greatly from others, so I will be quick to note that some folks have no qualms about earning money from entertaining others with their bodies. Although I think that there are better ways to earn money (I guess I'm not a rock 'n roll rebel), I know it's just my opinion. Some adults have no problems with taking their clothes off to entertain others with modeling, pornography, or prostitution. However, I am reminded of the conversation I had with a young lady at church years ago. She shared that she "used to strip and do nude pics" to support her drug habit. She said that it made her feel "so dirty and degraded." She said she felt like just a body. She felt like "a piece of trash, just discarded and thrown away." However, after she became a Christian, her faith made her feel convicted about her nude modeling and dancing, so she quit. She came to believe that her body was a sacred temple for her spirit and that her body "should be respected and saved" for her future husband.

The aforementioned is just one example of how entertainers can sometimes regret their work, or at least feel forced into doing it because of their circumstances. Folks are often obligated, or made to feel obligated, due to contracts that they signed without carefully reading or considering those contracts first. One of my favorite bands from my teen years, *Dead Milkmen,* reminds listeners of this with the words "The record company wants to sign your band. Watcha gonna do? Do the brown nose! Do the brown nose!" Hard rockers *Life of Agony* reminded listeners on the album "River Runs Red" to "Never, ever, compromise and you will never live a lie. Remember where you came from." Just read some of the interviews that I've included in this book. You'll see just a few examples from the thousands of musicians I've spoken with about how life as an entertainer ain't all glitz n' glamor.

Lastly, I am reminded of a show that I just had to be at in Knoxville. My favorite thrash metal band during my teenage years, *Anthrax,* played and my friends *shadowWax* opened up for them! I had just moved to Warner Robins, Georgia to start my job working for the Georgia Department of Labor as a Vocational Rehabilitation Counselor. It was in that December of 2003 that I received an email from shadowWax telling me they were opening for Anthrax. Instantly I began to celebrate, but the excitement quickly ended when I came back to reality.

Due to my recent move I was financially broke. Further my "work car," the '92 Grand Am I mentioned earlier in the book, was on its last legs with over 200,000 miles on it. My mom and stepdad had just graciously loaned me the money and paid for me to move to Georgia, plus have my car towed behind the moving truck from Knoxville. AAARRRGGGHHH!!! "I must be there!" I thought. But how was I to do it??? I did some checking on bus tickets and found a round-trip Greyhound "for 68 or less." *grin* But, I didn't have any money. Or did I??? Search James! Scrounge! Check the sofa cushions! Donate blood! Where would I get the money? I finally figured it all out. All I had to do was eat Ramen noodles, cereal, peanut butter sandwiches, and drink tea for a week, plus use my plastic magic wand (credit card)! *Hee-hee*

Okay, so I didn't have to go through the traumatic as I had foolishly planned to. At that time, I was receiving food stamps, because my income at Walmart before my Department of Labor job qualified me for them. Whew! What a relief! However, at that moment I didn't have anything left on my EBT food stamp card. Further, nobody took food stamps then or does now for a bus ticket. Oh, how my heart ached! In my mind, that was an incredible life-changing event, and since my friends were opening I had to be there with them to meet Anthrax and maintain "my reputation." *laugh*

Getting to the point... The next day favor came upon me. I know

now that God shines on me everyday, but at the time I thought it was part of his divinely appointed plan for me to get infected by Anthrax. *smirk* Like going to the show was going to help me... Anyways, I checked on my EBT card. The money came in! It had enough on it to feed me for a month! Yipee!!! I quickly got a bus ticket and made arrangements to stay with my friend Adam at his house. So, what about concert tickets? Who needs those when you're poor, but handsome like me, and your friends "get you in?"

The Grand Am definitely did it's job and drove me to Macon, Georgia where I left it at the Greyhound Bus Depot. That evening, my uncle David and his friend Johnny met me in Knoxville at the bus station to pick me up for the show, and of course they got in free too, along with Adam. Well, I just knew I would get to meet all of Anthrax and hang with them backstage, because after all, it was me, the most impoverished talent in journalism! So, after meeting and hanging out with the first openers *Straight Line Stitch*, and seeing shadowWax and Anthrax play great sets, the show was over and Anthrax's lead guitarist for this tour, Rob Caggiano, was hanging out with folks for photos and autographs.

Anthrax's longtime lead shredder Dan Spitz had reportedly left the band, shortly before this show. Therefore, Rob was filling in. Eventually, Rob returned to Anthrax to become the permanent lead guitarist at the time of this writing. He played great that evening and I got to meet him, plus have my photo made with him. No disrespect to Rob, but at that time I thought "this guy's just filler." Who cares who he's played with? I wanted to meet the rest of Anthrax. I was told they would be hanging around meeting people afterwards upstairs in the VIP area where folks like me were at during the show. Well, I was told WRONG. I waited around inside like I was told and soon learned that the rest of Anthrax was outside doing a meet n' greet at their tourbus and they had already hit the road and left town! Now when I recall all of this, I look back and grin with laughter. It's too funny! I couldn't make this stuff up if I tried! Furthermore, Rob Caggiano was, and still is, an excellent guitarist.

A few years later I saw him in a video playing guitar for Anthrax's song "We've Come For You All" when I watched MTV's "Headbanger's Ball." That's a great song and video! Rob Caggiano rules! My point is this: It didn't matter who Rob played with or whether or not he was in any videos or on any Anthrax records. He was a very nice guy when I met him, and I now consider him to be a valuable part of music history. I shouldn't have been such a "groupie" and reacted the way I did. After the show, I road home with David and crashed at his place in the mountains of Polk County, because Adam couldn't give me a ride to Athens. The next day David drove me to the Greyhound bus stop in Athens, Tennessee where I got on the bus wired with elation and a smile ten miles wide as I anxiously road my way back to Macon, Georgia. I had done it. I was still the coolest entertainment journalist in Knoxville. When I got to Macon, my ride was there at the depot waiting. It started right up and I drove back to my new apartment full of boxes and yummy Ramen noodles.

CHAPTER THREE

Letters

With this chapter, I decided to take various articles and pieces I've written such as CD reviews, concert previews and reviews, letters to artists, interviews, and similar, and compile those items into a chapter. Basically, this chapter's pages are examples of writings that I have done. Some of these writings were from works previously published in newspapers or other forms of media. Some articles have been altered so as to abide by copyright laws and general rules of etiquette. The first item is an interview with the "heavy industrial" band known as Ministry. I conducted it during the writing of this book for *Target Audience Magazine*. I was particularly interested in Ministry as this was supposed to be the group's last world tour.

Getting Ministered To:
A Farewell to Music Legends
by
James Hester

Those who appreciate fierce, heavy, industrial music need to pay homage to synth-metal pioneer Al Jourgensen and his often imitated band, of crass nonconformists, Ministry. After 27 years of pummeling the minds and ears of listeners, the technological beast known as Ministry is saying farewell on its final world tour to support its two most recent albums *The Last Sucker* and *Cover Up*. The band has eleven full-length studio albums including four Grammy nominations. Three of the group's albums have sold more than 500,000 worldwide. They are *The Land of Rape and Honey* (1988), *The Mind is a Terrible Thing to Taste* (1989), and *Filth Pig* (1996). Ministry's *Psalm 69* (1992) has been certified platinum with more than a million sales worldwide.

Burton C. Bell and John Bechdel graced Target Audience Magazine with a candid interview, just minutes before performing to a capacity crowd in Atlanta for the "C U LaTour." Readers might recall Bell's powerful work as the guitarist for Fear Factory and Bechdel's commanding presence with Killing Joke as a keyboardist. The two were recruited by Al Jourgensen to perform on the two latest Ministry CDs, and also to be a part of the band for its final tour. The following is some of what they said prior to their onstage circus manifesto:

TAM: Who or what are some of your primary influences?

JB: Early keys. Early synth and keyboard rock.

BCB: Early and post-punk British new wave. Obviously Ministry. We love Al and all of his work. It's an incredible honor to get to play with him.

TAM: With the politically-charged nature of Ministry's music, does the band endorse any particular parties or candidates?

JB: Al's always rooting for a Democrat. Al tried to get things set up so so he and Ministry could perform at the Democratic National Convention, or at least be there to support the party, but it never materialized. He has his preference for candidates, but they are almost always Democrats.

BCB: I don't really care for either party, but Bush has ruined this country (America) so far. I mean, we tried the first time Bush got voted in.

TAM: Or won by court decision.

BCB: Yeah, I'm not even sure who won that election. I think Al Gore might have been a good president. We tried in the first election, but got a raw deal and then there was the second election and neither party had a good candidate. I mean, the Democrats didn't have anybody. There was no one in the second election who could beat Bush. All they had was Kerry. None of the candidates in that election were worth it, but Bush had the money to pull it off.

TAM: Since your band's name is Ministry, do you consider yourselves ministers of any particular faith or philosophy?

BCB: It's a political office in England.

JB: I think Al said the name came from a movie.

BCB: It has nothing to do with religion. It's a title, like "Ministry of War or Ministry of Finance."

TAM: What advice do you have for indie artists to be successful???

BCB: Uh…Try a different career. (laughter from everyone)

BCB: No, seriously. If you're in this business for the money, you're in it for the wrong reason. My advice is for people to go to college and get their educations. Study hard and be a doctor or a nuclear engineer, but don't try to become a star.

TAM: So, how do you guys make money in this business?

BCB: In general, the band makes more money off of selling merchandise than anything else. We do better from selling CDs, music online and in stores, and stuff like shirts and posters than we do from tickets, because the money tends to be more residual and the amounts we earn are more consistent than from ticket sales.

TAM: Is it fair that a certain company is buying up radio stations and clubs across America and monopolizing the popularity of only select artists?

BCB: No. It sucks. People were so sick of that company, that I think they changed the name. But hey, a turd by any other name is still a turd. It's just the nature of corporate greed, or anyone really, to maximize profits and cut losses.

JB: Yeah, but they're brainwashing all of the kids by programming them to listen to their crap. It's just something else you deal with if you want to work in the music industry.

TAM: So, was it fair to go after Microsoft, but to not go after others for being a monopoly?

BCB: No.

JB: No.

TAM: So what do you guys like to do with your free time?

JB: I just like to relax and get some peace and quiet alone at home. At home mowing the grass is good for me these days. Afterwards, just sitting back and sipping a beer. We stay busy playing loud music and performing, so we tend to want to have some "down time."

BCB: I like to jam on my guitar and listen to the latest tunes.

TAM: So, who are some of the artists you're listening to right now?

BCB: I've got three right now. The new one by Nick Cave, but I like all of his stuff. The soundtrack for the movie 30 Days of Night. The Kills. Lots of stuff really, but those are some of my favorites.

TAM: Speaking of favorites, what are your favorite songs to play live?

JB: I like to play old blues. Stuff from the 60s. Stuff with keyboards.

BCB: Thieves. I absolutely love playing that song. It just flows so well and it really clicks. It's a great song to jam on live and I'm glad Al recorded it.

TAM: What reason most influenced your wanting to work with Al Jourgensen?

JB: We're huge fans of Ministry and Al Jourgensen. I mean it's another notch under my belt. Al's work has been such an incredible influence on the heavy and electronic music industries.

BCB: It sucks really that Ministry is retiring, but I respect Al's decision. I love his music. I listened to Ministry before and after I had joined Fear Factor and it still inspires me.

TAM: What influence do you want Ministry's music to leave on the world for present and for future generations?

BCB: None. No...

JCB: It's a way to contribute politically. We want it to be a way we can share our thoughts and dreams and provoke others to do the same.

BCB: Yeah. Living the dream.

JCB: We do it for the music. It's kinda what we do.

The band is calling it quits after a trilogy of CDs (2004's *Houses of the Mole*, 2006's *Rio Grande' Blood*, and 2007's *The Last Sucker*) dedicated to its disapproval of President George W. Bush and his administration. Frontman Al Jourgensen has stated that he likes "the synchronicity of Dubya and Ministry riding off into the sunset hand in hand." After our interview, Target Audience Magazine also spoke briefly with guitarist Sin Quirin who had been delayed and was unable to be part of the interview. He shared that Atlanta was one of his favorite cities to perform in and was very optimistic and enthusiastic about his work with Al Jourgensen and his career with Ministry. Our own Lucky Martin was on the floor center-stage in front of the band to savor the craftiness and cleverness of Ministry's last performance in Atlanta. Read his review of one of music's most relentless and tenacious groups on other pages in this issue.

I really appreciate my good friend Ellen Eldridge of Target Audience Magazine allowing me to publish this article in my book. As I mentioned earlier in the book, Ministry was one of my favorite bands during my high school years. Killing Joke and Fear Factory were also favorites. Al Jourgensen has been a big influence on my own music. At the time of our interview, Ministry had four Grammy nominations. Shortly after our interview the group had its fifth nomination for a Grammy with its recording of the Rolling Stones' classic "Under My Thumb." I also want to give thanks to Julie Arkenstone and Heidi Fitzgerald for helping arrange this interview for me. Angelina Jourgensen has my thanks for approving my use of the photo of me with Ministry in this book.

August 23, 2007

Honorable President George W. Bush
1600 Pennsylvania Avenue, NW
Washington, DC 20500

Dear Mr. President,

I know you have, perhaps, the most important job on Earth being the leader of the greatest republic humankind has ever known. With that said, I can appreciate your responsibilities and the value of your time. However, I am compelled to write you with questions during the midst of some challenging times in America. You have publicly addressed the concerns of human rights and equity in our global neighbors, but what are you doing to assure that Americans will continue to have equal opportunities to lives, liberties, and the pursuits of happiness? Should not our own citizens be protected first under the Constitution? What are you doing to encourage American businesses to employ more Americans instead of their hiring non-American-citizen laborers? When will you stop allowing foreign labor to work in America, or in American owned companies abroad, without being taxed?

Currently, non-American citizens are pouring into this country, but are not paying taxes on the wages they earn. There are corporate demigods hiring and exploiting cheap foreign labor, but those entities do not pay taxes on their foreign employees either. How is this situation fair to America and its citizens? The gulf between the wealthy and the poor in America is widening. How is it fair that many African-American families, whose ancestors helped to build America under the bondage of slavery, cannot obtain credit and loans as easily as some non-citizens? Is it fair that those migrant workers are allowed credit and loans through their employers who do not pay taxes on them? Corporate greed, along with America's lax border security, is threatening to destroy America.

I know America is a nation of immigrants, and I applaud its diversity. America's economy may have grown under your administration Mr. President, but for whom? Who is receiving the rewards resulting from America's overall economic growth? To further complicate things, you have obligated Americans to serve in a war they did not begin. If the US military is not protecting oil and American assets, what is it protecting? What has America gained from the war in Iraq Mr. President? I am a person living with disabilities and receiving Social Security benefits. I graduated college with honors, and earned a scholarship every year, but I am currently under-employed, and I have been under-employed since March 2006. What are you doing to ensure equal employment opportunities, and to reduce discrimination in America for persons with disabilities and others? I appreciate your answering this letter Mr. President, and you are in my prayers. May God Bless you, and may God Bless America.

Thank You,

James W. Hester
-------------------Dalton, GA 30721

I published this letter because I never received a reply from President Bush, in spite of my having received the certified mail receipt back from the White House. I know that he is a busy man and was President of the United States, the greatest nation on Earth, but I was disappointed that I did not receive at least a form letter back from him or one of his representatives. I include this letter in my book to show readers that I am a concerned citizen and I try to live an informed life. The vast majority of people can only begin to imagine the enormous responsibilities and pressures associated with being a celebrity of such caliber as The President.

Ike Dirty Interview
by
James Hester

As Target Audience Magazine strives to support and expose artists, it particularly wants to draw attention to those in its home city of Atlanta. With that said, Target Audience recently caught up with producer and entrepreneur Ike Dirty at the Atlantis Music Conference. Although he is actually Isaac Hayes III, son of the late soul crooner Isaac Hayes, Ike's work speaks for itself and the man's work stands on its own. The list of artists and clients he has worked with include: Ying Yang Twinz, Chamillionaire, KeKe Palmer, voice overs for McDonald's, the Atlanta Falcons, Publix, American Airlines, Cadillac, and cartoon hit Aqua Teen Hunger Force. Perhaps, his best known recent work came when he produced the colossal hit "Money in the Bank" for Lil' Scrappy. In between hosting discussion panels and his daily work, the artist and multi-platinum selling hip-hop guru graced us with an interview.

TAM: So, where are you from originally?

Ike: I was born in Memphis, but I grew up in Atlanta and I live here now.

TAM: Who are some of your influences?

Ike: I've got a lot of R&B influences. Quincy Jones and David Foster's work is good. I like Dr. Dre', Organized Noise, and Outkast too. Obviously my father. A lot of stuff influences me. I listen to all kinds of music.

TAM: You're kinda like most musicians. You listen to a little of everything right?

Ike: Exactly.

TAM: So, what predictions, if any, do you have for the music industry?

Ike: Oh man! It's so up in the air! Every day history is being made.

TAM: In Music?

Ike: Yes! Not just in music. I mean everywhere!

TAM: Do you think music in general is too negative nowadays, particularly for youth?

Ike: No, not anymore than it was when we were growing up. I mean there's always problems and there's always going to be controversy. What artists say and do with their music is a sign of the times. It reflects. The economy, the war in Iraq, gang violence, and illegal immigration are just some of the reasons why the content in music might be dark or controversial.

TAM: What trends do you notice in current music or do you see coming?

Ike: I have noticed that it seems to be more advantageous for companies and music labels to keep producers sort of "in-house." I see Chris Brown being put with boutique staff.

TAM: Boutique staff? What do you mean?

Ike: I mean that rather than contract out to record producers, labels are beginning to have their own producers signed, just like musicians, because their work is art too. Now, when a label records a group it will put that group with a particular producer whose style is similar. You know? One (producer) who is familiar with a certain style of music and who has experience recording in that genre.

TAM: What are some of the steps you take in the recording process?

Ike: I basically have five steps:

1. Get familiar with the artist. LEARN THE ARTIST. I try to bring the best records out. I try to become as familiar with a music as I can. I learn about their backgrounds, how they grew up, where they're from. That's stuff's important. I want listeners to be able to know and feel the artists I record.
2. Recording and producing used to be a pigeon-holed process. Artists would be forced to go with whatever the producer gave them. They didn't have a say, they just worked with it. I'm not that way. I definitely tailor the production and recording sounds to the artists I work with.
3. I usually use Logic and Pro Tools recording software on my computer. It helps me edit.
4. Again, as I said before, music is a sign of the times. I try to produce music that is relevant.
5. Educate yourself. I try to be knowledgeable about everything.

TAM: Because knowledge is power?

Ike: Yes it is!

Immediately following the interview with Target Audience, YouTube Raps arrived and its host Denocka Wardrick was standing by to get commentary from Ike Dirty about his experiences at the Atlantis Conferences and about the current music scene. Ike signed some autographs for fans, including this writer, and was cordial. Incidentally, as Ike Dirty and his publicist Dee Dee Cocheta, of A.B.C. Associates, walked with us to the interview location folks often stopped him along the way, shook his hand, and gave him their respects and approvals. His down-to-earth persona and approachable demeanor made Ike Dirty a popular part of this Atlantis Music Conference.

My thanks go to Target Audience Magazine and Ms. Dee Dee Cocheta for hooking me up with a great interview with such an interesting music icon.

Topaz Review

Velour Music recording artists Topaz are "smooth operators" on their current release *The Zone*. Listeners may remember hearing the ensemble open for jazz guitar virtuoso John Scofield at Blue Cats here in Knoxville. This CD masterfully blends East-coast jazz standards with Latin beats and funky disco arrangements to create a mellow treasure of sound. The band opens with a fluid tick-tock drumbeat and horns reminiscent of those on 70's TV cop shows like *Starski & Hutch* or *CHIPS*. In the tune "Minha Mente" is a voice chanting "In my mind…" as the band pours their souls into the music. The next song "I Can See It In You" is a happy story about the gift of friendship and having a good time with someone special. It is a good mood setter and an accurate reflection of the group's live sound due to its lively beats and chorus horn parts.

The third song "Walkabout" is a dramatic suspense builder similar to scenes where the detectives drive about slowly at night in their old Plymouths hunting for the bad guys. It definitely has a classic style complete with thick, phat bass lines, keyboards, whah-pedals, stereo chorus, and saturated with reverb and a slick production. Wonderful movement is created in the song with the clear, crisp, and syncopated drums keeping a steady rhythm behind the meandering crescendos of the horns. The next song "4th & D," slows listeners down with a light and somber instrumental. The tune sails gently through a stream of scales gradually building its tempo along the way to a danceable beat, and then gently returning listeners to calmer waters. The band continues their odyssey in the tune "You & Me." It is another item that aids the listener in creating a relaxed ambience as the band incorporates an echo effect on the vocals and carefully orchestrates horn scale arrangements.

Next, is the song "The Zone." It begins lightly with drummer Christian Urich brushing the symbols and quickly builds into a roaring funk inferno. This song opens with very clean sounding guitar strums. It develops into an eclectic barrage of fusion saxophones complimenting Ethan White's Wurlitzer organ. The complexity of Topaz' musicianship is evident as the guitar and keyboards rely heavily on electronic effects such as whah-whah and reverb. Again, this piece articulately reflects what the band might sound like live. Track number seven "Naked" has a very tribal feel and begins with African woodwinds and drums. It starts slowly, builds into a frenzy of lively horns, and returns to soft serenity. Topaz ends its CD with "Fat City Strut." The song introduces itself to listeners with a guy yelling the songs' title. It has a sound and feel that is very reminiscent of the godfather of soul James Brown and his work. Every instrument and every part of this song is masterfully arranged by Topaz. It contains more traditional horn parts than the others and it ends with a man's facetious laughter. In closing, this CD is highly recommended. Its songs were well-written and the production was superb. For a serene moment of positive energy, check out "The Zone." Grade: A+

Many thanks go to Jenn from Velour Records for giving me Topaz' CD and asking me to review it. I thoroughly enjoyed hearing the band live and getting to meet them. This CD is one of the best in my collection. At the time when I received this CD, Topaz was on tour with legendary jazz guitarist John Scofield and I was a guest for the show. This article was published prior to this book in *The Daily Beacon Newspaper*.

Interview with Sir Mix a Lot

After an incredible performance at The Pub, legendary rap and hip-hop artist Sir Mix-A-Lot pleasantly surprised me by inviting me onto his tour bus for an interview. It was the Grammy winner's first and only performance in Knoxville, Tennessee. I was surprised because I had not scheduled a meeting with him ahead of time. One of his crew members chatted with me after the show and graciously asked if I would like to interview him. It felt like a dream, but Mix-A-Lot quickly reminded me of just how real it was with his friendly demeanor. Upon entering the bus, he humbly stretched out his hand and said "Hi, I'm Anthony." Sir Mix A Lot, born Anthony Ray, had not lost his modesty as he quickly removed his black Stetson hat and invited me to his hotel room for an interview.

Upon arriving with my entourage (Eric Davis and Cyrus Lloyd), I tapped three quick knocks on his door, hoping I wasn't waking someone else up at 3:00 in the morning. Immediately, a muffled voice behind the door asked: "Who is it?" I stated my name with enough volume to penetrate the door, and quickly Mix bellowed out "Hold on a minute dawg, I'm takin' a shower!" What a relief! I sucked in a breath of fresh air and grinned like a schoolboy during recess. Waiting for the man was never a problem. The Radisson Hotel was nice and well-accommodated. Besides, his crew was in a room across the hall relaxing and just hanging out. David Doyle, an Events Coordinator from Absolute Entertainment, stepped out of the party and chatted with me while Mix finished his shower. He said Sir Mix-A-Lot was "the most down to earth" guy he had ever booked for a show.

Shortly after listening to David's insightful comments, Mr. Ray graced us with his presence. He asked Cyrus, Eric, and me to follow him outside to his tour bus so he could "get some clean drawers." As we walked I told him I was impressed by his modesty and lack of arrogance. He said "You gotta keep it real, and keep it real don't mean keep it thug." He quickly expressed his disdain for rappers that glorify violence and thug life. He said "Rappers singing about murdering people who try to take their females and their drugs are bull. Anybody who really did that would be doing time." Anthony furthered cleared the air by explaining his musical hiatus. He said he didn't really care about being popular. He had his fortune and fame and had "nothing to prove to anyone." Mix recorded and produced five albums from 1988 to 1996. Recording legend Rick Rubin (who has worked with Slayer, Beastie Boys, Danzig, L.L. Cool J, Johnny Cash, and The Black Crowes to name a few) was the executive producer on those works. In 2000, he released a best-of compilation of his work titled "Beepers, Benzos, and Booty: The Best of Sir Mix A Lot."

His first recording *Swass* contained less political rhetoric than those that followed, but contained a surprisingly good rendition of the Black Sabbath classic "Iron Man" performed with the 80s thrash-metal band Metal Church. Mix's multi-platinum selling hit "Baby Got Back" was banned by MTV after its video release in 1992. It was perceived by some to be racist, sexist, and derogatory against women. However, fellow rapper Chuck D of Public Enemy convinced Sir Mix-A-Lot it was worthwhile and should be recorded. Mix said people need to "learn not to misunderstand artists." He explained that the Grammy-winning song was about how "women don't need to be skinny and anorexic in order to be beautiful." He reinforced that sentiment by saying that his mother made him promise not top call women derogatory names. However, he obviously appreciated women when he stopped during the show and asked "Doesn't Knoxville have any ugly women?" as several crowded around him on stage and playfully "let it bounce."

When asked who his favorite female recording artist was he said "Alicia Keys is real." Other favorites he cited were Metallica, Bubba Sparxxx, Public Enemy, Creed and Slipknot, but he said he likes all kinds of music. He said he was strongly turned onto rock and metal after meeting Metallica at the Grammy Awards in 1992, an event both performed at. Fans might remember Mix's work with fellow Seattle artists Mudhoney in the song "Freak Momma" featured on the 1993 *Judgment Night* movie soundtrack. It was a case of where hip-hop met grunge in a common theme: women. Mr. Ray said his "goals constantly change." Currently, he is an independent producer for rock and metal bands. Recently, he has worked on music with The Presidents of the U.S.A. in a collaboration titled *Subset*.

Sir Mix A Lot recently appeared on the VH1 special "100 Greatest One-Hit Wonders" along with many other unforgettable artists. In spite of not having several "hit" songs, his music has forever captured the attention and respect of those in the hip-hop music community. Besides facetiously rapping about females, Mr. Ray addressed serious issues as well. His 1988 sophomore release *Seminar* included "National Anthem," an angry rhyme about the Iran-contra scandal, the American drug crisis, and the plight of Vietnam veterans. In 1991 Ray released his Grammy-winning, multi-platinum-selling work *Mack Daddy*. Its first track "One Time's Got No Case" was an angry response to racist police officers. It was to some as controversial as the record's third track "Baby Got Back." On his 1994 album *Chief Boot Knocka*, he expressed a displeasure for the Internal Revenue Service and its conduct, and how he was fed up with that system on the song "Take My Stash." In that song he warned listeners about living "too large, cuz' the IRS is gonna take your stash." In the song "What's Real" Mix A Lot tells the story about a young Black male growing up in the hood during the 1970s. Also on that album is the cynical tune "Don't Call Me Da Da." It's a song about a woman's infidelity and how she tries to tell a man that the child is his, when he knows all too well that it isn't.

Anthony continued to make "bootiful" music with 1996's *Return of the Bumpasaurus*. On that album he reminded listeners to be true to themselves and not forget their roots, particularly on the song "Aunt Thomasina." It's about how a woman lost her modesty after going from poverty to becoming conceited and wealthy. In closing, Sir Mix A Lot was the most friendly and down-to-earth rap artist I have ever met. He masterfully expressed himself with intelligent humor that helped pave the way for hip-hop's culture and popularity. Long before Tupac was using wah pedals and talk-boxes in tunes like "California Dreamin'," Sir Mix A Lot had already perfected the craft. The poetic pimp wearing a Stetson hat and long fur coat may not be as popular now as he was earlier in his career, but his music will forever remind listeners to "keep it real."

This interview with Sir Mix A Lot is my favorite out of all that I've done as a music journalist. Mr. Ray was so friendly and such a gracious host for our interview. I wish him the best and hope he enjoys reading this book.

James Hester - Staff Writer
Tuesday, July 16, 2002 issue

The flat-key tunings and monstrous, locomotive rhythms of Jerry Cantrell are coming to Blue Cats here in Knoxville. Tonight, the world-renown guitarist and songwriter will showcase his talents for what is expected to be a club crowded to its capacity. The artist is best known for his work with the Seattle rock band Alice In Chains. He made his major debut twelve years ago on the band's Columbia Records release *Facelift*, which contained the smash hit "Man In The Box." In 1991, he showed listeners that acoustic guitars could still be heavy on the popular EP *Sap*. However, it was his work the following year on the group's second full-length album, *Dirt*, that propelled him into mammoth stardom.

Classic riffs and chord progressions in the song "Them Bones" bludgeoned the ears of listeners. The whiny vocals were complimentary to explosive shifts in tempo on the radio hit "Angry Chair," and the MTV hit "Rooster" told the story of a young soldier walking through a battlefield trying to not to get hit by enemy gunfire. His work continued with Alice In Chains in 1995's release of the EP *Jar of Flies* which contained the smash "No Excuses" and the soulful, somber ballad "Heaven Beside You." His final recording with the group came in 1996 when they released a CD of their live performance on MTV's Unplugged. His solo work debuted in 1998 on the album *Boggy Depot*. It expressed spiritual perspectives by Cantrell on the song "Jesus Hands" and contained the popular radio tune "Cut You In." This evening's show will expose new material by the artist from his recent self-titled CD. The new CD is on Roadrunner Records and features former Ozzy Osbourne and Suicidal Tendencies band member Rob Trujillo on bass and drummer Mike Borden formerly of Faith No More. Unlike his earlier work, the new has a more metal sound and a dryer overall tone. Also, the guitar arrangements seem to be more complex and tend to have a faster tempo.

Blue Cats manager James O' Neill said this event is going to be "huge." "I think it's really going to be a Blue Cats moment," he said. Promoter John Emerson of AC Entertainment assured fans that this concert will "rock like no other." Jerry Cantrell's last performance in Knoxville happened ten years ago at the Civic Coliseum when Alice In Chains opened for Ozzy Osbourne on his "No More Tours" tour. The artist will be meeting with fans and signing autographs today at the Disc Exchange on Chapman Highway at 3pm. Tickets are available at all local outlets and are expected to sellout. Fans are encouraged to purchase tickets early. Doors open at 9:30pm and the show is expected to begin at 10pm.

It was cool to see Jerry play with Alice in Chains when I was in high school and then ten years later get to meet the man whose music I have admired for so long. It was great to meet him! He's an interesting fellow and I hope the current Alice in Chains lineup has as much success as the original did. This article was originally published in The Daily Beacon Newspaper while I was in graduate school at The University of Tennessee in Knoxville. Check out my review of Jerry's show following this article.

James Hester - Staff Writer
Friday, July 19, 2002 issue

As expected, Tuesday night's Jerry Cantrell concert brought a capacity crowd to Blue Cats. Listeners were treated to an unexpected bonus when Gone Blind opened the show. The Houston-based band's sound swept the audience with a tsunami of thick, resonating rhythms similar to those of bands like Helmet. The second opener, Comes With The Fall, shifted the beat and introduced listeners to tunes that were more melodic and less distorted. The band's frontman had an intriguing presence, with an Afro that made him look like Jimi Hendrix and vocals that were reminiscent of Lenny Kravitz. The set ended with an announcement that the band would be back soon, leaving many under the assumption it was going to play a second set. Indeed, Comes With The Fall returned for a second set with a pleasant surprise. The band brought Cantrell onstage and revealed that it was his band for the tour.

Cantrell and his entourage opened with the song "Psychotic Break" from his new album *Degradation Trip*. After slapping listeners' ears with roller coaster emotions, Cantrell continued with another new song, the extravagant "Bargain Basement Howard Hughes." The band then slowed things down with the soulful ballad "Angel Eyes" and expressed mellow sentiments with "My Song" from Boggy Depot. With the radio hit "Anger Rising," Cantrell slapped listeners with an angry story about a boy growing up in an Alabama trailer park with an abusive father. Next, he performed "Cut You In" and continued shredding the airwaves with "Mother's Spinning in Her Grave." Blistering riffs erupted from "Spiderbite," a song describing drug abuse. Of course, the artist made the show complete by playing songs that made him a commodity when he was a member of Alice In Chains. The band performed "Would?" "Down In A Hole" and "Angry Chair" from the platinum-selling album. *Dirt*.

Following a frenzy of audience singing, Cantrell returned with the dirge "Hellbound" from his latest album. Before ending the event, he wrapped the audience in "Chains" again with the melodic "Heaven Beside You." Lastly, Cantrell performed his first hit song "Man In The Box" from the Alice In Chains album *Facelift*. Afterwards, members of his band shared their thoughts about the show. When asked what he liked best about working with Cantrell, drummer Bevan Davies said it was that he "made a new best friend" in the guitarist. Bass player Adam Stanger said he had especially "enjoyed working with the new techs." He said it was the first time he had been to Knoxville, and that performing here had been a blast. Cantrell's tour manager Jim Runge said the band is currently on tour with Creed, but in between arena shows the band performs at clubs like Blue Cats. Cantrell will next be in concert with Creed at Nashville's AmSouth Amphitheatre on Aug. 17.

Oh my! I thoroughly enjoyed this show! I got to speak with Jerry after the show as well, but off the record. Jim Runge invited me to come

up to Nashville and hang out with Jerry and company as a guest for them and Creed, but ultimately I had other personal obligations such as graduate school at the University of Tennessee that I had to tend to. This review was published in the Daily Beacon Newspaper as well. Special thanks to Jerry Cantrell for being so cordial while dealing with (at that time) the recent passing of Alice in Chains singer Layne Stayley.

Cookie Cutter Girl Review
by
James Hester

American music history recognizes Massachusetts as a bastion of great music. Aerosmith, Mighty Mighty Bosstones, Boston, and Godsmack are just a few of the successful artists in recent years to hail from that city. Lynn Julian is no exception. Introducing herself as America's "Pop Superhero," the Boston artist has created a source of inspiration and support for girls and young women everywhere using the Cookie Cutter Girl alter-ego. She presents herself as a comic-book icon dressed to look like some sort of 21st century Wonder Woman. Call it a gimmick, but it works. One cannot deny that Julian combines raw talent and creativity with a sensible and educated mind to help empower listeners.

Julian lived in New Haven, Connecticut until age 10, but then moved to Maine where, according to a conversation with this writer, she "grew up." Currently, she makes the Boston-area her home and base for the Cookie Cutter Girl concept. The motivated feminist shared that Cookie Cutter Girl was something she created as a result of numerous struggles and challenges she has endured since childhood. Her stated mission is "to help women and indie musicians feel more empowered. She said that her work is "more geared toward girls and young women."

There is such a stigma against women in the workplace, especially those who are professionals. We are expected to work hard, be smart, be productive and efficient, AND be sexy. I'm tired of the glass ceiling. Men dominate the world in terms of money and commerce. There is sort of an unwritten rule that if you are a woman, you can't be the leader of a successful business, without being pretty.

I want to dispel that notion. I know that early on when I wore some Cookie Cutter Girl costumes, I got complaints from some parents that I showed too much skin, so I covered up my boobs and my butt more. They didn't want their little girls dressing like sluts and idolizing a stereotype of what women are expected to be like. That's just it though, we are subjected to so many stereotypes everyday. I agree with them that little girls and young women should respect themselves and not feel like they have to dress or look a certain way in order to be accepted. I want to help girls and young women to become more empowered, so they can believe in themselves and know that they are beautiful and important just as they are. That's why I created Cookie Cutter Girl. –Julian

A shrewd artist and business person, Lynn Julian dreamed up and created Cookie Cutter Girl. She is a self-taught guitarist, but has also earned an associates degree in jazz and contemporary music from the University of Maine. The artist has been featured in Rolling Stone Magazine who called her "Nashville's version of Fiona Apple." She co-wrote her first comic book with Justine Fontes of Disney and Dreamworks. Her cookiecuttergirl.com website says that her alter ego is a "modern day Cinderella story." Her music is catchy, witty, pop that discusses a wide variety of issues women face in a tongue-in-cheek fashion. It is saturated with bluesy, folk-tinged, guitar-driven harmonies backed by Julian's warm vocals.

Currently, the artist is not touring with her band *Pop Superhero*, due to a recent fall and injuries sustained at one of her live shows. Instead, she is focusing more on developing her comic book, making appearances at comic book shows, and selling her merchandise. She recently won contests at Boston and New York comic book conventions for Cookie Cutter Girl. A poster of her band makes a cameo appearance in the latest *Ace Ventura Pet Detective* movie. Julian's website is a plethora of information and networking and contains several links supporting other artists, particular those who are independent. For more info about Lynn Julian and Cookie Cutter Girl, visit her website at www.cookiecuttergirl.com or look her up on MySpace.

Lynn Julian is a treasured veteran of the indie music scene. She has been a great supporter of my writing and a good friend. Be sure to visit her website and look her up on MySpace. This interview was published in Target Audience Magazine prior to being in this book. Support girl power! Support Cookie Cutter Girl!

Review of LB Collective
By
James Hester

The soulful, introspective sounds of Atlanta's Laura Benjamin and her group LB Collective are sure to charm listeners. With sounds and lyrics reminiscent of dames such as Fiona Apple and K.D. Lang, LB Collective's latest release *let it go* will capture the hearts of listeners who yearn for moody, abstract, melodies. The singer, pianist, and songwriter carefully weaves a variety of styles and genres into the fabric and substance of this CD. This album begins and ends sounding like contemporary, light, pop music, but in between the first and last tunes, Southern, country-fried, delicacies abound. The first song "Oblivion," has a funky, bluesy, feel similar to what one might hear in a smoke-filled lounge full of pool tables with patrons sipping on PBR while the wailing Benjamin suggests that maybe she should "fall into oblivion."

Track 5, "With us for Awhile," especially has the potential of becoming a classic country music hit due to is heavy reliance on slide-steel guitar playing and its twangy effects on the guitar. A standout is "Goodbye Pluto." A song with piano, lyrics, and vocals similar to Tori Amos as it tells a story about how it was wrong when some in the scientific community decided not to classify Pluto as a planet in Earth's solar system any longer. The last song "What Would He Think" is the story about a girl growing up and wondering what her late father would think and say about what she has become, and the vocals and style are similar to Celine Dione. Other musicians contributing to this delightful CD are A.J. Holz on bass, Steve Mounce on percussion, and Diana Mounce on vocals. This piece also features Doug Kees on guitar and Cameron Hizer on keyboards. Take a listen to this. **This Atlanta artist personally mailed me her CD! Check it out!**

The Autumn Offering:
"Fear Will Cast No Shadow"
by
James Hester

Seasoned fans of the metal genre and heavy music know that Florida has for many years been home to some of the industry's best. The latest release from The Autumn Offering is no exception. The album *Fear Will Cast No Shadow* features the group's new lead vocalist Matt McChesney and the new drummer Allen Royal in a well-produced collection of songs about the darker moments of life. Recorded and mixed at Audio Hammers Studios in Sanford, Florida, this piece is destined to become a classic for any who appreciate angst-filled, guitar-driven music.

The Autumn Offering successfully create a harmonious balance between elements of both classic and contemporary metal music. With arpeggios reminiscent of guitar god Joe Satriani, the band's melody is complimented by the warm, thunderous, machine gun rolls of a double-bass drum similar to Igor Cavelera when he pounded the skins for Brazilian thrashers Sepultura. The band intricately articulates its arrangements offering at times snarling vocals to compliment brutal guitar attacks and at other times clear lullabies to match the mellow flow of the carefully orchestrated musical scores. McChesney's singing is similar to hard-rocking peer Pepper Keenan of Corrosion of Conformity. The band's mixture of snarling death-metal vocals with mellow singing is similar to contemporaries Bullet for My Valentine or My Chemical Romance.

In closing, this CD offers listeners elements of influences from many styles and genres of music, but its guitars maintain the work's metal sound and feel throughout the eleven songs. Virtuoso guitar playing and a crisp, clean sound, hold the listener's attention. The rolling thunder of the drums combined with the blistering, heart-pounding riffs takes each listener on a ride not soon to be forgotten. Often, when a band changes its lead vocalist, many fans are lost as the sounds and styles change also. However, fans of the Autumn offering need not worry about the excellence of this album. For more info visit www. theautumnoffering.com or the label at www.victoryrecords.com

Autumn Offering were an excellent listen to. I am glad Performer Magazine sent me this band's CD to review. My review ended up being published in an issue of the Southeast edition of Performer Magazine back in 2007.

Spitting Out the Fun with Saliva and 10 years

Playing again to a sold-out crowd, Saliva soaked the ears of listeners with their homegrown mayhem. It was the second time the Memphis-based rock band had headlined a show at Blue Cats. Like the first show, fans crowded into the courtyard and filled the club to its capacity. The event, sponsored by 94.3 Extreme Radio, was host to some of the genre's best from Tennessee. Local radio celebrity Roach hosted the evening and started by demanding everyone "make some noise" for Knoxville's own 10 Years. The band slowly entered the stage in what was either a ritual to introduce themselves to listeners or a cleverly disguised sound-check. It began with a soft, fluid melody that meandered its way into an incredible thunder of soul-felt rhythms, preparing rock's loyal for what was to come.

10 Years' frontman Jesse stalked the stage swinging his dreadlocks to and fro, occasionally taking hits from his bottled water for relief. The band performed tracks from its recently released enhanced CD titled *Killing All That Holds You*. Its six-track sophomore CD combined thick, fluid, rhythms with impassioned, soulful vocals in a sound reminiscent of the bands Tool, Incubus, and Helmet. As their CD title implied, the popular locals did not hold back the intensity of their heart-pounding jams. A brief intermission followed 10 Years, giving all who attended an opportunity to mingle in the courtyard and check out thousands of motorcycles in town for the *Honda Hoot* rally. The evening's festivities were enhanced by Honda coloring the Old City with bursts of thunderous fireworks. As before the intermission, Blue Cats quickly filled with a massive hard-rock party. Roach told fans "these guys don't need an introduction" and applause rolled through the venue like a Sherman tank full of rock soldiers as Saliva entered the stage.

In a style classic of a Southern gentleman, Saliva frontman Josey Scott briefly introduced himself and the band telling folks that they had just returned from Europe and the Northern U.S. He continued, by saying he appreciated Southern hospitality and that it was "good to be home." The crowd roared with approval, cuing the Memphis marauders to hit the lights and pummel the crowd with the 2001 radio classic "Click, Click, Boom!" Scott and his entourage came to Knoxville in support of their third CD release *Back Into Your System*. From that album the group performed several radio hits including "Always," prompting lady listeners to buy t-shirts with the words "I Love You" printed on the front and "I Hate You" printed on the back.

Reflecting upon his recent international travels, Josey briefly shared his disapproval for Saddam Hussein telling him "this is for you!" The band evoked a passionate patriotic spirit with the songs "Pride" and the movie hit "Hero" from the *Spiderman* soundtrack. The band's beats were as acrobatic as the comic book super-hero when it showcased its rock prowess on the club's new larger and louder PA system. Blue Cats became an indoor arena when the rolling thunder of drummer Paul Crosby was backed by the snake-shake rumble of bassist Dave Novotny, and accented by the crisp, dry melodies of guitarists Chris Dabaldo and Wayne Swinny. Saliva's tall, bearded frontman continued his spirited assault by challenging fans to shake their fits and get "off the floor" with the anthem "Raise Up." After driving fans on a high-octane "Doperide," Saliva ended its jam by inspiring the crowd with the smash "Superstar," as Josey commanded the imaginations of listeners. In closing, Blue Cats manager James O'Neill said the club plans to continue charming fans with such world-class music by adding a new upstairs level to the venue that will allow patrons to look down upon the stage while artists perform. This concert may be the largest rock show Blue Cats has hosted to date.

I wrote this review for my good friends at 94.3FM in Knoxville to post on the station's Internet site. At the time, local favorite 10 Years was just starting to get popular and garner more attention from various media and the folks at Universal.

Neil Supports Memphis

Recently, Performer Magazine caught up with the consistently busy music enthusiast Neil Heins. As a native of Memphis, Heins has been exposed to great music most of his life. His appreciation for good tunes and good times, prompted the man to open the renown Memphis venue *Neil's* in March of 1993.

Neil's offers "a little of everything," said Heins. The popular club hosts shows in all music genres, but specializes in classic rock from the '70s and the 80s by groups like Mountain or Molly Hatchett. The Memphis Blues Society sponsors shows there the first and third Thursday of every month, also. Mr. Heins said his establishment also plays host to many jazz musicians as well, but carefully added that he supports "all local musicians," and everyone is welcome at Neil's.

Neil's holding capacity is "about 500 people." It boasts a 4000 square-feet stage. For booking, prospective artists should phone (---) -------- and ask to speak with Neil, or with his sound technician Richard Butler. This popular attraction is located at:

I wrote this short little piece about one of the great Memphis clubs. Neil Heins and Richard Butler were great to speak with for this piece which was published in the Southeast edition of Performer Magazine. Thanks guys!

BEALE STREET CARAVAN
SUPPORTS MEMPHIS MUSIC

Recording artists and music professionals in the Memphis area have the opportunity to share their work with listeners worldwide through a clever program. Co-producer Sam Tibbs said "Beale Street Caravan is the largest syndicated blues program in the world." According to Tibbs, the radio program is broadcast even in non-English language dominant countries such as Japan, Germany, and various African nations. The non-profit organization helps to promote both signed or independent blues musicians.

The more-unique aspect of Beale Street Caravan is that all of the music it broadcasts is "live." Tibbs explained that his organization seeks out live blues performances, for one-hour length programs, each to be broadcast separately for a total of 40 shows per year. Typically, bands will submit recorded work and promotional items to Beale Street Caravan, and its staff will collectively listen to the work and decide whether or not particular artists should have their work aired on the program. Its staff includes Executive Producer Sid Selvidge and Host Pat Mitchell.

After Beale Street Caravan's staff has chosen a group of artists for play on its show, that particular group is contacted and arrangements are made to broadcast its members. The organization travels to performances in various locations, and sets up equipment to broadcast from those venues. Tibbs said each performance his organization airs is recorded. "We record live-only," he said. Beale Street Caravan assists artists by helping to pay for their broadcasting fees and royalties earned. To find out more about how Beale Street Caravan can help promote individuals or groups of blues musicians, contact this organization by visiting its website at www.bealestreetcaravan.com . Artists can phone (---) -------- for further details or for general email send inquiries to:

info@bealestreetcaravan.com

I am so glad I learned of this great and worthwhile program in Memphis, Tennessee. Hopefully, they will continue to support blues artists worldwide!

On December 17, 2004 I interviewed Brent Smith of Shinedown at the Coca Cola Roxy Theater in Atlanta. At the time, the original lineup of Shinedown was intact and touring to support its debut album "Leave a Whisper." I promised Brent I would publish this article, but I don't think it ever ended up in print. Some readers might be thinking "James! How could you? How can you not remember for certain?" Well, I know I tried. Welcome to the exciting reality of free-lance journalism. I solicited various local papers and magazines. I heard back from the *Atlanta Journal Constitution,* but I know I was insanely busy with my work at that time. My bud Danny went with me to that event and the Armstrong Twins met me there as well. Danny's friend Andrea Ashby was the professional photographer for that show. I somehow got busy and lost touch with Brent and his reps at Atlantic Records and In De Goot Entertainment. I'm sure there are no hard feelings and everybody knows that the life of a rock star is always busy.

Interview with Brent Smith
by
James Hester

James: What is the best thing about being a celebrity?

Brent: I'm not one. I'm really not. I'm a musician.

James: Well, then I guess I can't ask you what the worst thing is then!

(chuckles from both)

Brent Smith proceeded to share with Danny and I, off-the-record, about all sorts of frustrations he was encountering at that time. Brent was optimistic and friendly, but at the same time he was honest and direct. He gave us a clear view of how work as an entertainer was not always glamorous. In respect for Brent and Shinedown this author will refrain from publishing certain portions of our interview.

James: How do you feel the recent violence at shows will affect things for future entertainment events? Things like Dimebag Darrell and Great White?

Brent: It won't change things. Clubs are gonna be ran the way they've always been. Bands are still gonna play dumpy little holes with lax security.

James: Even after what happened to Dimebag and Great White?

Brent: I'm afraid so. I'm miss Dimebag dearly. He was a personal friend to me and Shinedown. He supported us greatly and helped us early on when Shinedown started. What happened to him is a tragedy, but I don't think it will stop people from playing in dives.

James: I never got to meet him, but everyone I know said he was a great guy.

Brent: Oh, he was. He was super nice. The guy had a big heart. He loved music and he loved people.

James: So, what about fire hazards such as what happened to Great White?

Brent: Man, I don't really know. I'm not an expert on pyrotechnics, but that show was a real tragedy. It seems to me that things could've been planned better, but flames and effects have been a part of shows for a long time and I don't see them going away.

James: At what moment did you realize you were living your dream and had made something of yourself?

Brent: Since I heard "Fly From the Inside" on the radio. After that it was just knowing that people liked my stuff and wanted to hear it. I'm so blessed. We played at Bogart's in Cincinnati and it's tough to sellout, but we did it.

James: Sellout?

Brent: Oh no, we didn't SELL out! We sold every ticket and filled that place! When I saw that, I knew the fanbase was growing. Another defining moment for me personally was when I got a phone call one day. I answered it and it was Sammy Hagar on the line. He said he really liked Shinedown and asked me if we would want to tour with Van Halen. I about fainted!

James: How has faith or religion affected music for each of you?

Brent: We're all pretty spiritual. Personally, I believe in Jesus Christ. The other guys in the band have different faiths, which you should ask each of them about personally. The record is about what we've been through. I'm not perfect, but I pray.

James: So, what's the best thing about working in the music business?

Brent: You should ask our manager Roy that question!

Roy: Sleep! Whenever you can get it is the best thing in the industry!

(laughs from everyone)

Brent and I had our interview prior to his going on stage to perform with Shinedown during the band's soundcheck and personal time. The show was excellent and the band Silvertide opened. It is the previous band for Shinedown's guitarist Nick Perri, whom I also met at this show, because he was playing for Silvertide that night. Before and after the show Brent and Shinedown were friendly and spoke with fans signing autographs and making photos with them. Just prior to processing and publishing this book, Nick Perri left Shinedown. I wish Brent and Shinedown the best regardless of who performs with the band.

Shedding Some Light on shadowWax
By
James Hester

Why all of the buzz about Knoxville? Hard rock band shadowWax has been touring Georgia recently in support of its latest album *Invitation Karma Crash*. The four-man audio train from Knoxville made a stop in the heart of Georgia at the Vinyl in Atlanta earlier this month. shadowWax is Eric Christopher on vocals and guitar, bassist Khhris Hamlet, guitarist Rocky Norman, and Beau Baxter on drums. After the band's performance its members reflected on their recent efforts and shared their thoughts about the current music industry in an exclusive interview.

Did any particular religious or philosophical beliefs inspire the latest CD's title?

Eric: *It's about how people think they can do whatever... I know that sounds clichéd.*

Khhris: *It's also about how people think things that are not accurate.*

Eric: *Definitely. People often view us in the wrong way. For example, we had some industry brass want to sign us, but only if we would alter our appearance and morph our sound into something like Matchbox 20. That's not us. We don't want to be like anyone else. We want to be ourselves, just shadowWax. I mean there's too many labels, but if you had to describe us I guess we would be equal parts a punk band and a rock band.*

You mean punk as in a way of life?

Eric: *Exactly! We embrace the punk philosophy, but we're basically just a rock band. It's a lifestyle. It's about being true to yourself and others.*

Khhris: *I could be playing anywhere, at anytime, and if I don't agree with something or someone I don't care who hears me say it's bull.*

Eric: *It doesn't mean we have to be disrespectful or mean, but we're not worried about being politically correct. Too many folks can't handle that. People can think whatever they want about us, but we know we always have a lot of support back home. We're going to be featured on the TV Show 'Live at Five' in Knoxville next week. We're also going to be making history next week as the first hard rock band to headline the Sundown in the City Festival. Even though it's usually mostly jazz, funk, country, and blues types of bands, we're not worried about critics.*

shadowWax has been around for a number of years, but the current lineup is not all of the original members. What made Rocky and Beau want to join the band?

Beau: *I used to be the drummer for another great band in Knoxville called Copper. shadowWax played numerous times with Copper, prior to my leaving them (Copper). At the time when Eric approached me looking for a drummer to join shadowWax, I had not touched a drum kit for two years.*

Rocky: *I don't know... I'm not sure really. I had mixed feelings about Eric at first. I saw him perform live and before I met him I thought 'This guy's a jerk.' But, then we met at another show and talked and it changed my mind about him.*

Khhris: *You wanted to be in the band, but didn't know it!*

Rocky: *Yeah, Eric's a good guy and I'm really glad I joined shadowWax.*

Beau: *It just seemed right at the time, I mean the timing was perfect for me to begin working on music again. I get along with Eric, Khhris, and Rocky really well and I wanted to experiment a little.*

Let's shift gears for just a moment. I understand that you guys are currently working on new material with award-winning producer Jeff Tomei. Eric has shared with me in the past that Alice in Chains and many of the bands from Seattle have been big influences on your music. Did that affect your decision to work with Jeff? How did you make that choice?

Eric: *Fate chose Jeff Tomei. Jeff is 100% heart. He's like my best friend. Jeff truly believed in shadowWax and has supported us from the beginning. In fact, he called me earlier today and we discussed the mix on a couple of songs. When we laid down some tracks with him and the brass told us to cheese-coat the sound, we said no, but Jeff was like 'It's cool. Just be yourselves and put this on the back burner for a bit till the industry is ready for it.' He said that things change and sooner or later the music will turn full circle and fans will be ready for us.*

I'm beginning to hear a bit of a theme within our conversation, and that's heart. It sounds like the band, and the people it chooses to work with, has a passion and a heart for music.

Khhris: *Yeah! You can't package that. We love what we do. Our van with the band's equipment broke down on the way to Atlanta and it took us like eight hours to get here. There wasn't anything special about that.*

Eric: *It's about the fans and the band.*

My up and coming book is about the entertainment industry. It's not always so glamorous. Behind the scenes there is a lot of work that goes into producing good music and entertainment. Entertainers often sacrifice more than the public will ever know.

Eric: *I agree. My biggest problem today is that most music is stale. I want to create movement. I want to tell a story.*

Rocky: *Yeah, we want to change music! We played at a club in Augusta a few days ago called The Mission. That show was great. Those kids were starved for rock 'n roll.*

They probably were ready to hear about something other than the Master's Golf Tournament.

Beau: *Yeah, the media just tells kids what they 'should' hear. It's great to see fans deciding for themselves what they want to listen to.*

One of the things I discuss in my book 'I Wanna Be a Rock Star Too' is demographics. Various folks at AC Entertainment, and others in promotions, have told me that it is sometimes difficult to market music in Knoxville, because there are so many talented musicians there playing many different styles. There's not just one particular scene to market. For example: Jacksonville has a lot of metal bands, Las Vegas has a dance scene, Detroit traditionally has rock, but Knoxville is more diverse.

Eric: *Again, we're not kissing up, but we do work very hard for our money. We felt very much at home playing The Mission, but one thing you can't do with rock music is get comfortable. If you ask me, I think the demographics in Knoxville have changed. Currently, there is a hard rock scene. A lot of great musicians have come out of Knoxville within the last ten years. Knoxville right now is like Seattle was in the 90s.*

Would you say Knoxville is experiencing a sort of 'musical renaissance' right now?

Eric: *Oh, definitely. So many great musicians have come out of Knoxville. Brent from Shinedown. 10 Years got signed. Brian from Weezer. The bass player for Three Doors Down, Jag Star…There is definitely a scene in Knoxville right now. We are very proud to be from Knoxville, because we get such tremendous support there.*

CD Review
By
James Hester

Recently, I had the good fortune of catching a hot up and coming rock band at the Vinyl Club in Atlanta. The band that caught my attention was none other than shadowWax. After the show, the band spoke candidly about its music and some of its aspirations. Following the intriguing conversation with shadowWax, the band gave me a copy of its most recent CD *Invitation Karma Crash*. After being treated with a great live show, my ears were very blessed when I gave the CD a thorough listening to.

The album begins with a song that shares its name with the CD's title. This first tune sort of sneaks up on listeners with only one guitar riffing a few bars in the right speaker, but the tempo starts to change when the rest of the band joins in on the left and quickly builds to a thunderous chorus. Upon hearing the first few measures of the band's lyrics, one might easily think he or she is listening to the vocals of the late, great Seattle rocker Layne Staley. However, the instrumental arrangements on this song tend to move faster and have a less melancholy theme than Staley's work with Alice in Chains. Also, the production tends to be a little cleaner and more digital than the more-traditional analog productions by musicians prior to the 21st Century. Lead vocalist Eric Christopher introduces the band's strength as he yells the chorus "Invitation karma crash... Nobody wants to go! All you smiling fools..." In the post-show interview, Christopher said the song was about how "what comes around goes around," and about how members of shadowWax have often been misunderstood by others. The song races atop a pavement of warm, thick bass lines, and avoids the hazards of being dull and cliché.

Next, the band shifts gears, slowing its sound and removing much of the distorted guitars and angst in the song *Downtown's Drowning*. The song opens quietly with Christopher singing lightly over choppy bars of piano chords followed by the soft viola slides of renown string virtuoso Erin Archer. The intro is reminiscent of a television or movie score. The fluid guitars and bass are reintroduced as the song steadily builds into the chorus "Downtown's drowning and it's overrated, it's complicating you." The vocals are cleaner and more polished on this song than the previous, incorporating more reverb and echoing effects than in the first song.

The band brings its quick tempo and energy back on its third effort *Survive the Fall*, but in a style that is more-contemporary and similar to

79

current hard-rock radio playlists. It opens with a blast of squalling fretwork harmonics by the band's guitarist Rocky Norman, whose picking drives the song and moves it forward into time and key signature changes. The song is a moody ballad in which the band encourages the listener to live through life's troubles, stopping "hopeless suffocating and hopeless screaming." Adding to the song's adhesiveness to one's senses is the combination of clean, fluid bass lines accented by dryly distorted rhythm guitar licks.

Perfect Disguise is orchestrated in a classic-rock style. Without the vocals of Eric Christopher, one might assume this song was recorded by AC/DC, especially with the guitar leads and arrangements, so reminiscent of Angus Young. It's simply a good old-fashioned song about being genuine or being fake. It reflects the diversity of the band's influences, because unlike the previous, it does not sound like most current music.

Next, the band lulls you with a dreamy tune that is full of melody and movement similar to groups like Smashing Pumpkins or King's X. It brilliantly moves through a story about finding oneself sailing through a turbulent sea of emotions. The echo effects and chorus vocals help paint an alternate vision of reality upon a canvas of gentle sounds. *In My Name* is dramatic and passionate as the band sings "dreaming myself to sleep" in fluid harmony. Trip on this, but without the hangover.

The sixth tune, *Lakeshore*, is a ballad about an emotionally troubled girl who is "lost again in herself." It begins slowly with moody guitar arrangements accented by warm, soft, bass lines and is reminiscent of tunes such as *Lovesong* by the Cure or *Black Lodge* by Anthrax. The song is also similar to movie scores in that movement is created as Eric Christopher cleverly narrates a story about a girl finding what she needs as the band plays lightly for several measures before suddenly jumping into a punchy chorus-break of distortion in which the song's main character is "falling to her knees." The title of this piece may be a sort of play on words, because in the band's home state of Tennessee there is an in-patient psychiatric hospital in Knoxville called Lakeshore Mental Health that is literally on the shores of the Tennessee River. Also, another in-patient psychiatric facility called Moccasin Bend is located on the shores of a river in Chattanooga.

The band returns to a more-catchy and radio-friendly sound on the song *Mostly Maybe*. Similar to fellow hard rock contemporaries the Foo Fighters, the song has thick, heavy rhythm guitars that are complimented by traditional meandering lead guitar licks. It's a happy little ditty that summarizes its theme with the words "if only for this moment."

Next, the band picks the beat back up and slaps listeners with an octane boost of *1,000 Fingers*. The phat bass work of Khhriss Hamlet and clearly accented beats of drummer Beau Baxter truly make this gem shine. The chorus "a thousand fingers today raining downward" describes a feeling of being the center of attention and having everyone point fingers at you. Eric Christopher reminds the listener to hold his or her "head up and break them all away." This song encourages listeners to be themselves and not cater to the selfish demands of others.

Uma Thurman's Motorcycle Pants rocks! Besides the witty title, the band of easy riders takes you on a romantic motorcycle trip along the lusty roads of a young man's affection for the beautiful and talented actress Uma Thurman. Guitarist Rocky Norman borrows a few licks from Mötley Crüe as this song opens with the guitarist making motorcycle noises on a guitar. The band gives listeners whiplash as it speeds toward a "deathwish in lipstick." The guitar and bass arrangements, and effects, on this song are similar to those found by female rockers L7 on their album *Bricks Are Heavy*. Following in the tradition of songs like *Iron Horse* by the band Mötorhead, this song is destined to become a classic piece of recorded art.

The final tune of this CD *Monday* is a mellow love song about how the song's character never had a good Monday until he met and fell in love with a girl who told him to "be still." It prompted a genesis of feelings for her that he never had before. This is another excellent example of shadowWax's musicianship. The bass lines and the arrangement of the choruses are very similar to classics by Led Zepplin or the Beatles. This legato number is gentle and ends the CD on a relaxing note.

In closing, *Invitation Karma Crash*, is an excellent album. The production is good and similar to that of currently popular artists. This album might be more appreciated by writers and musicians than by fans due to its eclectic themes and overall complexity. However, the band hopes to gain more attention and recognition when it completes its current work with award-winning producer Jeff Tomei. The band's lead singer Eric Christopher said shadowWax has been approached with numerous offers from major record labels, but the band is yet to find a contract it is satisfied enough with to sign. Perhaps, working with Tomei, who has produced artists such as Alice in

Chains, Smashing Pumpkins, and Jerry Cantrell will help the group secure a better deal.

Hopefully readers enjoyed reading this review and the one to follow about the band The Mule Thieves. This Mule Thieves review appeared in Southeast Performer prior to this book. shadowWax and The Mules Thieves are two of the best bands to come out of the Southeast U.S. in recent years. Please go out and support these worthy artists and continue to support all local artists and unsigned talents in your area!

Mule Thieves
by
James Hester

Here's a group that reminds me of why the dirty South is an excellent place for great music and good, clean fun. Fronted by Donovan Cox and John Stanek, The Mule Thieves hail from the beloved Southern rock town of Athens, GA. The CD's cover reports that all songs are written by Cox and all of the lead vocals are performed by Stanek. Like other Athenians who have impressed listeners before them, The Mule Thieves are destined for greatness if they will maintain the sounds they have on this CD. The guitars, bass, background vocals and programming are all the work of Donovan Cox.

The album begins with a burst of warm, chorus vocals backed by the thick, fluid rhythms of a resonating bass similar to the sounds of 80s icons Simple Minds or U2. Stanek's vocals on the first tune *Boiling Point* also remind this writer of fellow Southern-rocker Brent Smith of Shinedown. The third tune with its mandolin and violin arrangements is similar to renown Southern violinist Erin Archer and her work with Jag Star's Sarah Lewis on mandolin. Standout tracks on this piece include: *Space Cowboys* and *Winter's Passing*, an instrumental.

Perhaps, the most radio-friendly song, that would be good sold as a single, is the monstrous wailing of *Moonshine*. It is a high-octane rush in which Stanek blissfully sings the chorus "running through the woods never felt so good, never been this high drinking moonshine." All drums on this self-titled CD are performed by Chris McHugh courtesy of Sony Discrete Drums. Additionally, there are guest appearances by Benji Wilhoite on piano and on backing vocals. For those who like arrangements similar to those by Days of the New or Alice in Chains, check out The Mule Thieves.

CHAPTER FOUR

Captain's Log

With this chapter, I sort of wanted to do a journal. I was inspired to do so when I read the book "Broken Summers" by *Henry Rollins*. Mr. Rollins wrote the whole book as if it were just one big journal, with there being dates for each entry. It had a cool, classic-style, typewriter font throughout the book. I thought it would be great if I did similar for just one chapter, in order to give folks a better idea of how a "rock star" lives. I was very resolute for awhile and wrote EVERYTHING down. Then I got busy and procrastinated, thus giving readers this slop. *chuckle*

1. **Accepted Jesus Christ as my personal Lord and Savior October 1986.**

   It was sometime in October of 1986 when a guy named John Shelton visited Lovell Heights Church of God in Knoxville to share his testimony. He spoke of how he was an inmate on death row, but new evidence was found and he was released from prison upon overturning his conviction. That evening I learned how I needed Jesus and I got saved. Like a lot of kids, as I grew older I lost my faith in Christ during my teen years. I hated all churches and organized religion and saw it as a way to manipulate others. However, after being involved in a near-fatal car accident in 1994, I had a near-death experience. My Christian faith returned after having many of my prayers answered. My faith and personal relationship with God have both grown, and I am still growing better daily.

2. **Got engaged to Katie on February 15, 2008.**

   Katie and I couldn't get together and celebrate Valentine's Day on that Thursday, because she had to work that evening teaching music lessons. So, we had our date the next evening, of course. We went to a nice local Italian restaurant for dinner. After dinner, we went to Red Top Mountain State Park, which is where we had first met for a date. I had Katie close her eyes, as I had "a surprise." While they were closed, I pulled out the ring and while kneeling on one knee I asked her: "Kathryn Elizabeth Atkinson will you marry me?" Whew! I'm sure glad she said yes! I was SO nervous. You just don't want to mess up such important questions! I had finally found my partner for life.

3. **Got married to Katie on March 15, 2008.**

The State of Georgia requires couples receive counseling before marriage. We went to our church pastors and got the required amount of counseling. Both Bishop Stephen Thomas (my church) and Reverend Ross Wiseman (her church) each agreed with us and asked the same question "So, what are you two waiting for?" We had a small ceremony with just our parents and a few immediate family members at Community Fellowship Church where I was a member.

4.   **Charlie Daniels Band with Buddy Jewell. October 15, 2004.**

I first met Charlie and his band at the Georgia National Fairgrounds in Perry after a coworker's sister got me a backstage pass, because she worked in the industry for another popular country music entertainer. Originally, I had planned on meeting him a few months prior in Atlanta at the HiFi Buys Amphitheater with Wynona Judd, but my friend who had the passes in her name got sick and was unable to go with me. I arrived and the venue gave me the tickets at the "roll call" window, but since the tickets were not in my name I was not allowed to meet Charlie. However, Charlie's people were very cordial and friendly and they still put me in VIP seats in front of the stage. A few weeks after enjoying the show in Atlanta, a friend hooked me up with a backstage pass for the one in Perry. Don't worry folks. I bought a ticket for my brother Tim and I to go to this show. I'm really not a conniving cheapskate. *grin*

It was incredible! While waiting in line for Charlie during the "meet 'n greet," I met a DJ from a local radio station. After chatting for a few minutes, he graciously gave me a pass to meet the opening artist Buddy Jewell. Both Charlie and Buddy were great to meet! I invited each of them to stop by *Faith Promise Church* in Knoxville, where I was a member. My brother Tim arrived late to the show, because he had driven from Tennessee on his way to Florida to visit some friends at the University of Florida in Gainesville, so he missed Buddy Jewell. We were both blown away by the musicianship and diversity of Charlie Daniels and his band. Charlie and company actually played some jazz, rock, and gospel songs that night. Tim said he was impressed, because he thought Charlie's music was just gonna be "twang." Like true rock stars, Tim and I left the next morning and drove down to Florida to meet up with some friends of his and hangout. 'Cuz it's Tim's world! Tim's world! Party time! Excellent!!!

5.   **Met Mike "Action" Jackson in Dalton, GA. Spring 2007.**

I met this wresting superstar a few times at a Walmart in Dalton, Georgia where he would sometimes set up tables and sell his videos, plus set up a wrestling ring outside for matches. As I understand it, he did this in part to raise money for various charities and church groups he helped support. In his hey-day, he wrestled against many greats including the "Nature Boy" Ric Flair. Mike has trained thousands of pro wrestlers through the years and is well known in the business. One of his trainees was former star Marcus "Buff" Bagwell whom I mention later in this chapter. I have to say that I was thoroughly amused and entertained when I watched Mike play the part of an angry bad guy one afternoon in a match at Walmart. It was hilarious! What a great performance! It was so funny to watch an otherwise mild-mannered nice guy turn into an obnoxious, trash-talking freak. His memorable match reminded me of why my brothers and I loved to watch wrestling as kids. You can't help but laugh at it!

6. **Blue Note sax player Karl Denson. Fall 2002.**

My "partner in crime" Eric Davis and I got into this show as guests. We learned that Karl had played sax for Lenny Kravitz and others, but I was more impressed by Karl's performance. The man was INCREDIBLE! He was also on one of my favorite jazz labels *Blue Note Records*. After watching Karl tear things up on the sax and on the flute, Eric and I chatted with him and had our photo made with him. Karl was a super nice guy when we met!

7. **Quiet Riot with Wall Street and Dancing with Ellie. July 9, 1992.**

Read about me meeting these bands in a previous chapter. As it was one of my favorite bands during childhood, I was thrilled to meet Quiet Riot!

8. **1982 World's Fair in Knoxville.**

I remember going to this sometime in the fall of that year, because it was cooler weather. There was all kinds of cool stuff to see and do at the World's Fair. I remember a giant Heinz 57 ketchup bottle robot rolling around and dispensing little green pickle pins to folks, and I got some. I remember hearing the song "Photograph" by *Def Leppard* jamming in the background. I'll never forget playing with toy cars that had steam engines and ran on water. They had little "gas canisters," and I took the canister of water and put it in the tank of the car when it ran out. Folks were entertaining ideas of alternative fuels even way back then! We need to use such innovative technologies now!

9. **Jag Star with Seamus Tierney. Knoxville, Tennessee 2000.**

Jag Star eventually became a popular band from Knoxville and got sponsored by major labels. I first learned of them back in 2000 when I saw the lead singer as I was walking out of the Tennessee Theater in downtown Knoxville. I knew Sarah, because she was in my my homeroom my first year of high skull at Central. We were both leaving a show from one of my all-time favorite funk bands *Gran Torino*. A short time later I went to one of Jag Star's shows with my cousin Cyrus. He knew the group's violin player Erin, because he used to be a neighbor of hers when they were kids. Anyhow, we saw them play a few times with drummer Seamus Tierney. Seamus was incredible and we knew of his work featured in *Modern Drummer* magazine. He had played with many artists including Tori Amos and Letters to Cleo at the Lilith Fair Festival prior to pounding the skins for Jag Star.

10. **Johnny Cash. 1985.**

Again, I mentioned meeting this awesome music legend in a previous chapter of this book. However, I was a kid at the time on a field trip to the *Museum of Appalachia*. He is one of my favorite recording artists now, but I didn't know who he was then. I often think of him. I actually cried when I learned of his passing away. He may be with us no longer, but his music lives on.

11. **Sir Mix A Lot. October 2002.**

"Don't nobody go messin' with my game plan, ol' Mix done, done it again!" Anthony Ray you're great! It was a pleasure meeting you for an interview. The article and a letter I wrote to Sir Mix A Lot can be found in the previous chapter. I had a great time hanging out with Anthony. For me, it is my favorite of all of the interviews I've written. Out of respect for the artist, I didn't take a camera with me to the hotel room he was staying in.

12. **Anthrax with guitarist Rob Caggiano. December 9, 2003.**

Ha! Ha! Rob Rules! I've only spoken with Rob briefly for a few minutes, but he was so cordial and friendly when we met. I enjoyed listening to him play live and seeing him in the video for the song "We've Come for You All." I mention the whole event in a previous chapter of this book. Hopefully, I'll get to meet the rest of Anthrax later. I talk about this earlier in this book. READ IT!

13. **Benji of Good Charlotte. 2002.**

We were at a club in Knoxville and we literally bumped into each other. Of course we both said "Excuse me." I'm not sure, but I think we were at Blue Cats. He started chatting with me and told me he was from Charlotte and sang for the band *Good Charlotte*. He seemed like a nice enough guy, but I had never heard of his band at that time. Honestly, I just started talking with him, because he had a cool mohawk that I found intriguing. I believe the bands Van Dyke Brown and Limit 9 were playing that evening. Well, a few months later I was getting buff in the gym at Tennessee Wesleyan College. Many of the students were MTV junkies and I looked up at a TV and saw Benji and his mates jamming! It was funny, because in the middle of my crunches and situps I blurted out "Hey! I know that guy! That's Benji. We met!"

14. **Producer Scottie Hoglan for Dolly Parton and Left Foot Down. 2002.**

My good friend John Montgomery played for great band called Left Foot Down. I was one of their groupies, heh...heh... Well, he invited me to come and hangout with them while they recorded at a studio in Knoxville. It was SO cool. I met Scottie Hoglan and took some photos. Scottie was also a guitarist for a Christian hard rock band called *Nailed*. I later learned that during the same week I was there with Left Foot Down, Dolly Parton stopped by and made some recordings. Included during her sessions was the *Led Zepplin* classic "Stairway to Heaven."

15. **Sevendust with Breaking Point and Element 80. August 26, 2003.**

Lejon Witherspoon is a really mellow dude. Totally relaxed! I first met him as a guest when Sevendust played at Blue Cats. He invited me and my friend (top secret) to come hangout as guests the next night in Johnson City, Tennessee at the club Rafters. After the first night when I met Lejon, my friend and I went to the hotel where the bands Element 80 and Breaking Point were staying. They were great to spend the evening with as well. After the next evening's show at Rafters, my bud and I crashed at my cousin Angela's house on our way back to Knoxville.

16. **Seether, Our Lady Peace, Shinedown, and Three Doors Down. 7-24-03.**

As I wrote previously in this book, my friend Brent Smith and his band Shinedown were the reason why I attended this show. I was a guest and I met all of the bands who played that night. My good bud from Oak Ridge High and UTK, Mike Woodward, hooked me up with press coverage. He was doing layout and design work for the *Knoxville Journal Newspaper* then. We were both at UT when I wrote for the University paper *The Daily Beacon*. Therefore, I was granted an interview with Brent and Shinedown which was published in the Journal a few days later!

17. **Powerman 5000 and Sloth. September 2003.**

I mention this show in a previous chapter of this book. Powerman 5000's drummer Adrian Ost is a great drummer and has been featured in numerous magazines including *Modern Drummer*. He was really funny when we met and was very sociable. I was impressed by him. Sloth were really a funny group of guys with dread-locked hair from California. Their manager was really cordial and gave me their CD to review and contact info. Brian Parsley snapped some nice photos of me with Sloth. A Bartender named Kirsten snapped a few photos of me with Adrian. She worked at Blue Cats and I was told by the manager that she had just won a Miss Hawaiian Tropic contest. Thanks for the photos Kirsten!

18. **Jerry Cantrell and Comes With the Fall. July 16, 2002.**

I had seen Jerry with his band Alice in Chains when its original lineup opened for Ozzy Osbourne in October of 1992. He has been one of my favorite guitarists and songwriters since I first heard him when I was in high school. It was especially cool that I was a guest for this show. My best bud Eric Davis and I got to chat with him both before and after the show. Although he was cordial and played incredibly well that night, I can remember a sense of sadness in Jerry that I am sure was somehow related to his friend Layne Stayley dying a few days prior. I wrote preview and review articles for the newspaper about this event. Jerry's manager at the time, Jim Runge, invited me to come and be a guest in Nashville for a few days later when Cantrell and his band opened for Creed. However, I was ultimately unable to attend due to my grandmother's (Hester) illness and other personal matters I was dealing with.

19. **Tantric with Shinedown. March 19, 2004.**

I was a V.I.P at this show and I remember it was very excellent. I got to hangout with both bands before and after the show. I made a special trip up to Knoxville for this show, because I wanted to see Brent and Shinedown again, since I had not been back to Knoxville since the Anthrax show the previous December. It was good to be back since having moved to Warner Robins, Georgia for my job. Along with the show, it was nice to see family and friends again in Knoxville. My cousin Cyrus came out to this show. I brought my newspaper article from when I first interviewed Shinedown and had all of the members sign it. Members of Brent's old band Dreve were there too and since bassist Andy Parks was mentioned in the article he signed it too. I mostly remember goofing off with Brad and Barry of Shinedown who kept teasing some groupie chick. Cyrus took a photo of me with Tantric's singer Hugo and his girlfriend.

20. **Drain STH with doubleDrive and Dreve. October 2000.**

This was one of my first major shows to write about. I published a photograph of me with Drain STH and wrote an article about Dreve in the first issue of my magazine *The V*üe. It was an incredible show and I had so much fun hanging out backstage with the bands. Brent Smith's old band Dreve opened at this event. doubleDrive were such cordial and friendly hosts. They really made me feel welcome. The ladies from Drain STH were great to chat with as well. I remember guitarist Flavia telling me about her preferences for guitars. Dreve were a local favorite and blew everyone away with its opening set. I heard this show helped industry reps from Atlantic decide to sign Brent Smith.

21. **Coal Chamber's Bassist. Rayna Foss-Rose. 2002.**

I was hanging out one evening at Blue Cats when we met. I thought she looked familiar, but didn't want to seem like I was hitting on her. She was cordial and told me her name was Rayna. She said she played bass for a band called Coal Chamber. I cannot verify for certain if I had met her at Blue Cats. If not, it was some blonde-haired gal who looked just like her and lied to me. Perhaps, she was impressed with the J-Dogg. *smirk* Oh well, if we didn't meet, then maybe sometime she can lay down some nice, chunky, bass lines on a few songs with my wife Katie and me! My wife is classically trained and has played with many orchestras. We should all get together and record a symphonic masterpiece!

22. **Switchfoot with Reliant K and The Supertones. 2000.**

I remember that sometime while I was a student at Tennessee Wesleyan College, I went to see all of these bands at Knoxville Christian Center. I went because of The Supertones. I didn't meet them, but after the show I did get to meet the two new (at that time) bands Switchfoot and Reliant K. Both bands signed my ticket and I still have it. Switchfoot went on to be a mainstream success. The date was printed on my ticket, but not the year. It was about 2000.

23. **Kenny Neal at 550 Riverside Blues. Fall 2004.**

I went to see this guy with my good friend Mike Avant. I had already seen him play bass with Buddy Guy in 2000 when they opened for B.B. King's blues festival. Mike lived in Macon and knew all about the guy. If I would've had my trumpet with me, I could have sat it, because Kenny invited me to do so. He had another fella with him playing keys whose name I don't remember, but he said he used to play with The Steve Miller Band and with Earth, Wind, & Fire. The place was packed like sardines. Good jams!

24. **K2S with The Insyderz, Deluxetone Rockets, and Miss Angie. 1998.**

I saw all of these excellent artists perform at Cleveland State Community College in Cleveland, Tennessee. I went with my brother Robert, because at the time he was living there and going to Lee University. It was a great show and we got to hangout backstage and talk with all of the musicians afterwards. I hope to see and hear more from these artists.

25. **T Bone from the movie The Fighting Temptations. 2000.**

It was a pleasure getting to meet this "street preacher" when he came to Knoxville. He has an incredible testimony of how God saved him from gangs.

I met him prior to his appearing in the movie "The Fighting Temptations" playing the role of a convict in a choir. It is an excellent movie featuring actor Cuba Gooding, Jr. T Bone signed my ticket after rapping his way through an excellent show of hip hop skills. I bought a CD and a bandanna from him.

26. **My next-door neighbor Mitch Rutman of Neil Young and Dave Matthews.**

I first met Mitch at a Gran Torino show. The funk supergroup filmed the show for a video. After hearing a great live performance, I mingled outside the club in the courtyard. Again, my "partner in crime" Eric Davis was with me. The reason I remember is because Eric asked him if he was Jewish. Anyhow, Mitch walked up to me and asked "Hey are you James Hester? Man, your name precedes you. I'm told you're the guy to talk to in Knoxville about getting press coverage for bands. My name's Mitch Rutman and I work for Dave Matthews and for Neil Young." My ego just about exploded at that moment. It's a writer's dream come true. Anyhow, a few months later in 2003 I saw Mitch in my apartment community and learned that he was my new next-door neighbor. He moved there temporarily before buying a house. Mitch is a great guy. He's really modest and down-to-earth. Last time I saw him, he was getting ready to open some shows for John Mayer and to play at Bonnaroo. He invited me to set in with him sometime to play trumpet, but we had some scheduling conflicts come up. I hope he has a lot of success with his music and working in the industry. This guy deserves a listen to!

27. **10 Years with shadowWax and Copper at Blue Cats. Fall 2002.**

I don't remember when exactly I first met all of these bands, but they are some of the best to ever come out of Knoxville. I have been to so many of their shows and talked with them so often in casual conversations that it's a challenge to recall all of the dates and times. Each band has received much radio play in Tennessee. All are great artists and each group has inspired me greatly. This evening when I saw all three together was incredible! My best bud from Central High Skull Patrick Morehead went with me. We saw my friend Holly Denman there and she is an incredible artist and illustrator of books.

28. **Bowling for Soup with Three Days Grace. Fall 2003.**

When I met these bands, they were just fresh and brand spanking new on the music scene. In spite of the odd names and the looks of these artists, I remember they were all so cordial and friendly. I did not know that four years later I would see Barry of Three Days Grace again and get him to sign the photo of us together. Rock on brother!

29. **Front page article for "Who Wants to Be a Millionaire?" Spring 2002.**

While I was in graduate school at the University of Tennessee and writing for the college newspaper, I was given the assignment to contact a student at UT named Katherine Hinkle in January of 2002. She was on the TV show "Who Wants to Be a Millionaire?" She had won $35,000 on that show. ABC and the staff of the Daily Beacon thought it would be interesting for students to read about one of their classmates in that context. The ABC network phoned me two or three times from New York and made the arrangements with me. My article was published in February of 2002. I felt like a million bucks after that!

30. **Bourbon Bowl Bash in the Fall of 2002.**

There was some kind of crazy party at Blue Cats to celebrate the rivalry between The University of Tennessee and the University of Kentucky's football teams. It was a V.I.P. Only event. People had to either be on the guestlist (like me) or had to win tickets from a local radio station. Radio DJ Mancow and his sidekicks Freak and Turd came and hosted the event.

31. **Todd Helton, Tony Cosey, and Bubba Trammel. All at Central High.**

I talk about going to school with these incredible athletes in the first chapter of this book.

32. **B.B. King Blues Festival with Buddy Guy.**

In September of 2000, my brother Tim surprised me with a great belated birthday present. He missed celebrating my birthday on August 25, so he got me a ticket and I went with him and some of his college buddies to this show. I forget who the artists were that opened before B.B. King. It was such a treat to see the legendary B.B. King live in concert at an outdoor amphitheater in Knoxville. He was so classy. I hope I can sit on a stool and play for thousands around the world when I'm B.B's age. Buddy Guy was phenomenal as well. His humor was thrilling as well. He had a wireless headset mic and a wireless on his guitar, so he surprised everyone by walking off the stage and out into the crowd between the isles. I met his bass player Kenny Neal in Macon a few years later. This show is a treasured memory.

33. **Cracker with LP. Fall 2002.**

This was the second time for my meeting Cracker. The first time was in 2000 at Moose's Music Hall for my magazine The Vüe. I got the assignment from the Daily Beacon to cover this show. Cracker played and excellent show! I've got a photo somewhere of Brent Smith from Shinedown at this show and he is standing in front of the stage looking at Cracker and wearing an Ozzfest t-shirt. I met the artist LP after she played. She gave me her CD and I gave it an excellent review which also got published in the Daily Beacon. Unlike the first time when I met Cracker, I got my photo taken with them this time. They are one of my favorite bands of all time.

34. David Wells of the Toronto Blue Jays on June 1, 1989.

My late father was good about trying to spend time with my brothers and I when we were kids. He got tickets and took us to an exhibition game between the Toronto Blue Jays and the Southern League All-Star Team. I met David Wells and he signed my program underneath his photo.

35. Tony Coelho of Al Gore and ADA. March 2003.

I talk about meeting Mr. Coelho in a later chapter of this book. He was a rock star to counselors and persons with disabilities for his working to help establish the Americans with Disabilities Act (ADA) of 1990. He was the President of the Epilepsy Foundation of America when we met. He also was a regular on CNN's show Crossfire. Prior to that he had managed Vice President Al Gore's run for the White House against "W" and he used to be a U.S. Congressman.

36. Three Days Grace with RED. November 17, 2007.

I went to this show first in Atlanta after a three month series of emails with RED's representatives arranging for me to meet with them for an interview. The venue was the renown Tabernacle. Due to scheduling conflicts, I was unable to meet with RED at this excellent show for an interview. However, the band was available at a merchandise table after it played and was chatting with fans and signing autographs. I initially met the wife of RED's lead singer Michael Barnes, and she was managing the merchandise table. She told me that RED's management had told them about me. *sweet* She said they were looking forward to doing an interview with me. So, after meeting Michael and company I confirmed it with RED's management and met with RED seven days later in Knoxville, Tennessee where they opened for the bands HURT and Seether. Ultimately, the band was delayed and arrived an hour late leaving me only able to interview RED's guitarist Jasen Rauch. Nevertheless, my interview with Jasen was excellent and was published in Target Audience Magazine. This show was where I met the band HURT for the first time. It was nice to see Seether again and to see them develop since I first saw them play in 2003.

37. Reggie White. The "Minster of Defense." 1982.

I was attending First Apostolic Christian Academy in Knoxville at this time and I was in first grade. I went on a field trip to Silver Dollar City in Pigeon Forge, Tennessee. I met Reggie White there and I remember hanging out with him a little and going around the park with him on rides. The reason I remember is because he was playing football at UT at the time. A black boy in my class whom I was friends with somehow knew him. That park later got bought by Dolly Parton and turned into Dollywood. My memory of this event is a bit fuzzy, but I usually don't forget faces. Later on at Northwest Middle School, Reggie White visited there a few times and we chatted. His aunt, Ms. Upton, was my English teacher. At the times when we met, he was "just some adult who played football," because I was just a kid. He was an incredible football player and minister, but he was down-to-earth and just an average guy. His aunt Ms. Upton was a cool teacher I remember and I enjoyed her class. Her contribution to my education makes her a rock star too!

38. Ashley Capps of AC Entertainment in Knoxville. Fall of 2003.

Prior to my moving to Georgia, I stopped by the corporate office of AC Entertainment (at that time) in Knoxville one afternoon to thank Amanda Tullos for helping me to interview Shinedown. My friend Carey Archer from the band Mr. Skinny was working there at that time also. Amanda told Ashley I was there. He personally came out of his office, shook hands with me, and thanked me for mentioning his company in so many articles I wrote. It was really cool to meet him, since he was busy being the President of AC Entertainment. Shortly after we met, he and his company became famous for the arts and entertainment festival known as Bonnaroo.

39. J Mascis of Dinosaur Jr. Met in summer of 2002.

This guy was legendary during my teen years for his work as a major independent recording artist. He is one of the pioneers of alternative music and culture in America. My bud Eric Davis was with me and we got our photo made with him. He's a great guitarist and has been featured in guitar magazines.

40. Melvin Gibbs of Project Logic and Living Colour. Met in 1999.

This guy was a cool cat when we met at the Tennessee Theater inn Knoxville. He laid down some nice, thick, bass lines for DJ Logic. Prior to his work with DJ Logic he played bass for Living Colour. We met outside of the doors that were entrances to the main theater. He signed my CD after we chatted for a few minutes.

41. Rock band Saliva. First met in Fall of 2002. 10 Years opened.

I don't know if my memory serves me correctly, but I think 10 Years opened for Saliva at both shows I attended. I have an article from one of the shows included in a previous chapter of this book. Saliva are from Memphis and 10 Years are from Knoxville. It's nice to see a bunch of Tennessee boys make it playing hard rock.

42. Played with Katie at Woodstock Coffee House. 1-24-09.

My wife Katie and I played at this cool local Coffee House in Woodstock, Georgia where our good friend Dale Capri hosts an open mic and sometimes plays there himself. There is an excellent menu here and a lot of cool artwork for sale hanging on the walls. Many great local musicians frequent this establishment. We were blessed with nice tips for only playing 2 ½ hours.

43. Minister Tony Campolo in the Fall of 1997.

I went to a conference with the Baptist Student Union of Hiwassee College during the weekend of Halloween in 1997. The "Crossroads 97" conference was held at the University of Georgia in the Classic Center. I met Dr. Campolo and spoke with him briefly about the Bible and faith. Years later he provided personal counseling for President Bill Clinton.

44. Interview with Brent Smith of Shinedown December 17, 2004.

I thought I was a big shot the night I did this interview with Brent in Atlanta, because I had two twin models with me as dates and my friend Danny Davis who had worked with Alice Cooper came along and got his friend Andrea Ashby to do the professional photography. We were at the world-famous Coca Cola Roxy Theater in Atlanta. Read the interview in the previous chapter of this exciting book!

45. Dickey Betts with Great Southern and JC Haun. June 13, 2002.

I was a guest for Dickie Betts and Great Southern back when I was in college, because my good friend J.C. Haun knew Dickie and invited me to the show. I talk about our meeting in the last chapter of this book, so you'll have to read further! Dickie signed my 1994 issue of Guitar World Magazine, because he was on the cover.

46. Miss Jahnnie. Met in Warner Robins in 2004.

I met Ms. Jahnnie at a restaurant she worked at when I lived in Houston County, Georgia. Her father Jae Moe played drums for The Allman Brothers. She was my server numerous times. I respect her privacy, so I won't say where I met her.

47. Congressman John Duncan, Jr. First met in August of 1989.

I had just gotten back to Tennessee from Virginia, because I was the bugler representing The Great Smoky Mountain Council at the National Boy Scout Jamboree. There was a flag raising ceremony held at the Monroe County Chamber of Commerce in Madisonville, Tennessee, because Congressman "Jimmy" Duncan donated a flag that had flown over the U.S. Capitol building to the chamber. I played the bugle call "To the Colors" at that flag raising. I got my photo in two local papers with two other Scouts who participated in the ceremony. I would mention their names if I remembered them.

48. **Mrs. Skaggs of Northwest Middle School. 1987.**

I mention Mrs. Skaggs, because I remember her telling me and my classmates that she was a relative of the country music star Ricky Skaggs. I never have listened to Ricky's music much, but I never forgot her telling me that. I really enjoyed her Social Studies class and liked her as a teacher. Perhaps, her helping me like social studies aided in my decision to minor in Sociology when I was in college. That makes Mrs. Skaggs a rock star too!

49. **The Wailers with The Uptown Bogarts. October 2001.**

I wrote a preview article for this show that was published in the Daily Beacon Newspaper. I knew Carrie Archer. He played keyboards for the Uptown Bogarts. They were a great jazz and funk group. The Wailers spent time talking with me after their set to discuss possibly playing at a festival that I was helping to promote. These reggae greats were good to talk with. Their trombone player asked me if I wanted to sell my King trumpet to him, because it was the kind he was looking for.

50. **Roscoe Orman of Sesame Street. 1986.**

My brothers and I were shopping at West Town Mall in Knoxville with our mother when I spotted Roscoe. I mention this event earlier in this book. It was cool to meet one of our Sesame Street favorites.

51. **Dreve with Alpha Zulu. December 1996.**

There were one or two other bands who opened for Dreve that night, but I don't remember who. I went to this show with my cousin Cyrus Lloyd after he told me about a great local rock band he had been following and talking to named Dreve. The show was at Moose's Music Hall on the campus of the University of Tennessee. It was Brent Smith's band prior to his singing for Shinedown. I remember liking Alpha Zulu, but I was completely blown away by Dreve. They were the best hard rock band in Knoxville at the time and I hadn't heard anyone as good from Knoxville in several years prior. Before the show ended I bought a Dreve demo tape. I got all of the band members after the show to sign the tape before they left. I told them all to keep playing and they would surely be successful. Brent Smith wailed on vocals. Hector Rodriquez shredded on the chunkiest guitar licks. Andy Parks maintained a thick, fluid, rhythm on bass. Drummer Eric Yarber rolled his way into my ears like a freight train with incredible double-bass work on the drums. My favorite song by them was "The Floor." DREVE RULES!

52. **Matt Hall and New Brutalism. 1993.**

I was good friends with Matt at the time and I had jammed with him once at Kevin Walford's house when he played with The Faction before changing the band's name. He went on to play bass with my friend Ben

Savage's (not the actor) band Flatrate. Matt is an incredible guy and I mention him earlier in this book.

53. Superjoint Ritual with Hank Williams, III 2002.

I remember getting the email about this show and I went because of Philip Anselmo and Hank Williams, III. I had not heard Superjoint Ritual prior to this show. I talk about this show earlier in this book. I learned an important and valuable lesson about stage diving. Go back and read it again!

54. Presidential candidate Lamar Alexander. Met at Duncan Family BBQ.

I talk briefly about our meeting in a later chapter of this book. I was invited to the Duncan Family BBQ in 2002, because I worked with Congressman Jimmy Duncan's sister, and also because my grandparents were friends with his father Congressman John Duncan, Sr. Therefore, I met former Tennessee Governor and Presidential candidate Lamar Alexander at this. Mr. Alexander formerly was also the President of The University of Tennessee in Knoxville.

55. Interviewed Sir Mix a Lot. October 2002.

I went with my cousin Cyrus Lloyd and my best Friend Eric Davis to a small place on the University of Tennessee campus called The Pub to see this Grammy-winning hip-hop legend. He was so friendly and cordial. I included an article about this event in the previous chapter.

56. Shim of Sick Puppies. June 2006.

I got an email about this event from my good friends shadowWax. They opened for Sick Puppies at a really cool festival in Downtown Knoxville that was sponsored by Yahoo Hot! Jobs. There were several stages around the downtown area with each featuring a particular genre of music. Best of all is that it was all free to the public. My uncle David and his girlfriend went with me and we had a good time. We also saw Mitch Rutman at the Preservation Pub on Market Square. It was the first time I had heard Sick Puppies. I chatted with Shim before his band played. Cool show.

57. Brian of Shadows Fall with Slipknot and Dixie Chicks Crew Chief. 3-19-05.

I went to this event upon the advice of the famous rapper / producer Sir Mix a Lot (Anthony Ray). When I had met Anthony and interviewed him, he told me about how he loved Slipknot and that I should go check them out. So, when they came to Hi-Fi Buys in Atlanta with Shadows Fall and Lamb of God, I was there! It was the "Subliminal Verses Tour." I stood in a V.I.P area with Brian the lead singer of Shadow's Fall and the Crew Chief of the Dixie Chicks (Sorry I don't remember his name). Brian was a very nice guy, but I didn't bug him for an autograph after his set because he was tired from his high-energy performance and I wanted to be respectful. I took a local neighbor's kid and I don't remember his name... (sorry).

58. Onya Richter of TBN. March 2007.

I met this local TBN station manager at my church in Dalton after I had played trumpet in a service that was later broadcast on the TBN network. She was very gracious and invited me to come and record at her studio sometime for free.

59. Bishop Harvey Bee. October of 2004.

I met Bishop Harvey Bee after my good friend and next-door neighbor Minister Damion Manwarren invited me to attend Christian Fellowship Church in Warner Robins, Georgia. Readers might remember seeing him on local cable television. Local people told me they saw me once on his show. I guess the camera liked me that day. *grin* Damion and Bishop Bee are both incredible evangelists and men of God.

60. Met former wrestling star Marcus "Buff" Bagwell. March 2008.

I met Marcus just after my wife Katie and I got married and moved to Cherokee County, Georgia. His website reported that he wrestled for WCW, but others have told me he also worked with WWE. He was a very nice guy and like his nickname, he was indeed buff. I met him at the gym my wife and I often go to, because he is a personal fitness trainer. Another personal fitness trainer Holly introduced me to him after we were discussing the paralysis in my left arm. He shared with me about how the world of professional wrestling entertainment is often grim and not as glamorous as one might think. He was in the process of writing a book himself and I told him I had some info about the deaths of many pro wrestlers in my book. Cool guy. Hopefully, we can trade books and help promote each others writing.

61. Canton Jones. Spring 2005.

I had the pleasure of hearing this smooth R&B artist perform at Christian Fellowship Church in Warner Robins, Georgia. I met him afterwards and he signed my CD. I later often heard him on local radio stations. Check him out!

62. Adion Hill. Spring 2005.

It is my understanding that my friend Minister Damion Manwarren helped arrange Mr. Hill coming to visit at Christian Fellowship Church. Damion introduced him that morning and said he had "won Grammy and Dove awards for his work." He used to direct The Colorado Mass Choir. That Sunday morning the Choir from Valdosta State University performed under the direction of Adion Hill. It was a phenomenal performance and I was blessed to meet Adion and shake his hand after the service.

63. I got Dumped for Jordan Night of New Kids on the Block in 2003!

I mean what he's got that I ain't got!?! Money!?! Good looks!?! Fame!?! Does he have a master's degree and a gold Beemer baby!?! This is just too funny and I had to mention it, because it's TRUE. I went out with this girl a few times who sang in the choir at a church that I attended. Anyways, some lady in the choir tried to play Cupid and introduced us. The girl also liked to dance and do choreography. Well, she broke it to me gently one evening that I was a great guy, but she had her heart set on dancing for Jordan Night and someday marrying him. I don't think that ever happened, because I casually spoke with her a few months later and she was dating some other guy, plus she wasn't working with Jordan. I've got no hard feelings and maybe she has worked with Jordan. It's just a funny memory, because I hated New Kids on the Block when I was in high skull. But I have the last laugh now! Ha! I'm married to the hottest rock star babe in the universe! Ha! I'm married to Katie! Ha! Ha! Ha! *grin*

64. Tonex' in Warner Robins with Christian Fellowship Church. July 16, 2005.

This cool-cat rapper performed at The Civic Center in Warner Robins. He was supposed to start hosting a new TV show on MTV for Christian artists, but I don't think I ever saw it. I met him and he reminded me of Michael Jackson with his dance moves. To further enhance his image, he wore an old Motley Crew t-shirt during his performance. This event was sponsored by my church. Nice show.

65. Missed meeting Ozzy Osbourne three times. 2001 to 2005.

I sure hope that one day I get to meet this rock and roll legend. The first time I missed meeting him was in October of 2001 when he was on his "Merry Mayhem Tour." He was scheduled to play in Knoxville at Thompson Bowling Arena with openers Rob Zombie, Mudvayne, and Stereo Mud. I had already spoken with a friend at local radio station 103.5 WIMZ and he was gonna hook me up backstage for this show. Well, Ozzy broke his leg and the show was canceled. It would have been his first time back in Knoxville since October of 1992. So, next chance was me meeting him at Ozzfest in West Palm Beach, Florida. It was September of 2004. I had tickets and I knew some of the bands on the bill, plus some of my cousins lived there and in Miami. Well, a bloody hurricane (in my best Ozzy voice) came through and the whole thing was canceled! Not just once, but the hurricane's eye passed over West Palm twice. I wanted so badly to go, because the entire original lineup of Black Sabbath was scheduled to play and this was the last U.S. Ozzfest date of the season. Oh well, so I planned to go next year to the West Palm Beach Ozzfest, because Sabbath was again on the bill. Curses! Another hurricane! Doesn't Mother Nature know that Ozzy said "you can't kill rock 'n roll?"

66. **Coco Beach. March of 2004.**

I wrote about meeting this group at Cocoa Beach and playing some trumpet with them. The account is written in the last chapter. The group included the drummer from Three Dog Night and the bass player for Ike & Tina Turner. Read the last chapter of this book to find out more. I was thrilled to jam with them!

67. **Michelle Snow of Women's NBA. Fall of 2002.**

I met this friendly basketball star one day while walking along the sidewalk on the campus of the University of Tennessee. I was working on my master's degree at the time. She was playing basketball for the university. I recognized her and said hello, because at the time she was the only woman in college basketball who would slam-dunk the ball. She gave me her autograph on a piece of notebook paper. Shortly afterward she got signed and joined the Women's NBA.

68. **Bass player for the Everly Brothers. Summer of 1992.**

I met this guy one afternoon when I stopped by Ciderville Music on Clinton Highway in Knoxville. The Everly Brothers were from Knoxville. At the time I was just some zit-faced boy who wanted strings for his guitar and "some old guy" chatted and reminisced with me. One of the workers at the store asked me "Son, do you know who this is?" I clearly did not know. He told me the gray-haired gentleman used to play bass with the Everly Bothers. I replied "Cool. That'll be the day, huh?" You never know who you might run into in a music-filled state such as Tennessee.

69. **Country Gospel artist Charlie May. 2007.**

I was eating pizza all alone by myself at CiCi's Pizza in Dalton, Georgia and this guy noticed that I prayed before I ate my supper. He asked me if I went to church anywhere nearby and we started talking. He came and sat with me at my table. Soon we became friends and hung out some. He gave me two of his CDs and informed me that he won an award for Country Gospel Songwriter of the Year. He showed me some stories for children that he wrote. He's a super nice guy and I wish him the best.

70. **The Shepherds. Met in October of 2005.**

I met this great Southern Gospel music group after visiting their church Kaolin Church of God in Sandersville, Georgia. Soon after I started attending there, they invited me to play with them at church during services. I had a lot of fun playing with these talented artists. They have performed on the DayStar Network at Kenneth Copeland's church and have been on radio stations nationwide for years.

71. Anointed with Zoe Girl in Knoxville. 2000.

I think I went to this show with my brother Tim. I went for Anointed, because I had seen them live in New Orleans back in 1998 at a Cross Seekers convention. Tim liked Zoe Girl. The show was cheap, which appealed to us as college students. Anointed was still great, but did not have a band with them like before. I really enjoyed listening to Zoe Girl as well.

72. Pirelli Tire Models in Atlanta car show March 13, 2004.

I met these ladies when I went to a car show with my good friend Mike Avant and his family. It was at the World Congress Center in Atlanta. I remember the model Linda told me her daughter dated the bass player for the rock band Yellow Card. She offered to help me get an interview with them. I appreciate her gesture, but obviously somewhere along the way I got busy and that interview never happened. Maybe that can change now...

73. Omega Rage at Hiwassee College in Spring of 1998.

This is without a doubt one of my favorite heavy metal bands! I went to college with the lead singer Josh's wife Rachel. I put an article about them in the first issue of *The Vüe Magazine*.

74. Disciple. Battle of the Bands. Maryville High. February 27, 1999.

My friend Jennifer Easter was the President of the Christian Student Movement at Hiwassee College, and through her I heard about this. We had a classmate named Rachel who's boyfriend Josh was the singer and rhythm guitarist for the band Omega Rage. Eventually Josh and Rachel got married. Disciple judged all of the bands in the competition. I met everybody in Disciple after Omega Rage won the battle and the competition was over for the evening. Awesome show!

75. Julian Drive at Crosspointe Worship Center. Spring of 2007.

I was attending this church in Dalton regularly for awhile and playing trumpet there with the musicians. One Sunday this awesome group of musicians visited there and played some of their songs. I chatted with them at their merchandise tables afterwards.

76. Elton Parks of Chaka Khan's band. Milledgeville, Georgia. Fall 2005.

I was at the "Second Batch Sweetwater Festival" in Milledgeville, Georgia on the campus of Georgia State University. I had just spent an hour on the tourbus talking with Blue Note sax player Karl Denson. I was hungry after chatting with Karl, so I walked across the street to a quiet little place called "Cafe South." As I walked through the front door of the cafe, I did a double-take when I saw this Black guy strumming some smooth jazz on a semi-hollow guitar. We both asked "Hey man, do I know you?" We shook hands and introduced ourselves. He told me he was Elton Parks and that he had just moved to Deep Step, Georgia from New York. He said he used to play guitar with Chaka Khahn in live shows "many years ago." A short time later, I played some light jazz on trumpet with him at the place where we first met. He's a cool cat. Nice conversationalist.

77. Spoke at and sang at a Hiwassee College convocation in Spring 1999.

I crooned some jazz and tried to be smooth like Sinatra at this event, but I don't think it really worked. Deborah Hicks was the Music Department's Director and she did an incredible job playing piano for the song I sang. I feel badly for the insecurities that I had when I was in college. I did want to share about my faith and praise the Lord Jesus Christ, but I also wanted to be seen and get the spotlight too. I wanted people to like me , because I felt like a freak due to my heavily scarred arm and terrible academic record in high school. I was still recovering from the car accident I was involved in when I was 18. I was also a high school dropout, so I needed a sense of accomplishment. I spoke at this convocation sharing about how I believe that God and His son Jesus did so much to help me. I want the world to know now that I want God to receive all honor and glory.

78. Moby with Dirty Vegas concert. July of 2002.

I wrote briefly about this show in a previous chapter. My best bud Eric and I got free tickets and went to this show at the Civic Coliseum in Knoxville. Moby surprised me by his having played guitar that night. I wish more folks would have come out to support him and Dirty Vegas. They are both excellent artists.

79. Performer Magazine. First issue was October of 2006.

I was working full-time at Broken Shackle Ranch as the Student Environment Coordinator when this happened. I also lived there on the campus of that facility. It was a ranch for assisting at-risk boys who were referred from the Department of Juvenile Justice or from DFCS. I went to Atlanta one day and met with the Editor Susan Wile-Schultz in person. It's an excellent mag that supports indie musicians. I got on board as a freelance writer for them. I did it mainly as another way to spread my name around, so people would know me when I released this book. I got several nice CDs free that I reviewed. Thanks Performer!

80. Mike Woodward. Met at the Golden Arches in October 1992.

I initially met Mike when I was slinging grease for the golden arches in Oak Ridge, Tennessee. I was 17 and we both skated at the time. I loaned him a few bucks one day and he paid me back partly with cash and gave me an Eric Smallwood skateboard deck by Basic. We became good friends after that. Nine years later we began talking again as friends when I started writing for the student newspaper at the University of Tennessee. In 2003, after having finished my master's degree at UT, Mike was working at the Knoxville Journal Newspaper. He helped me land a nice interview with Shinedown in 2003 when the band was touring with Seether, Our Lady Peace, and Three Doors Down. I owe a lot to Mike for helping me with getting my articles published for the Daily Beacon and for hooking me up with such a major article in my career as a journalist.

81. G Love & Special Sauce with Slightly Stoopid. September 2001.

I chose to cover this show out of a random pile of articles I had to choose from. I am so glad I did. At the time when I chose to cover G Love all I knew was that he was on Sony Music and I had seen him once in a commercial for MTV. However, my boy Easy D (Eric Davis) knew all about G Love and had been listening to him for years. Eric had seen him open for Dave Matthews at UNLV in Las Vegas. Eric "tripped without his luggage" when I told him we were on the guestlist for G Love. Eric had first seen G Love and Special Sauce with a crowd of about 20,000 fans. At this club show there was only about 400 fans and we got to meet Gordon "G Love" Duckett afterwards and got his autograph. He was a super-nice guy. Now he is one of my favorite recording artists. Slighty Stoopid thanked me afterwards for mentioning them in the article as the opener. Little did they know that years later in 2008 the same publicists representing Ministry would contact me requesting press coverage for Slightly Stoopid.

82. Sun Ra Arkestra. Fall of 2002.

These indie, jazz masters were sensational. Earlier in this book I wrote about my hanging out with them backstage. These legends have maintained their status as independent recording artists and Sun Ra would be proud of them if he were still with us. R.I.P. Sun Ra. Long live the Arkestra!

83. Acid Bath at the Mercury Theater. Summer 1996.

I was hanging out on Market Square one afternoon in Knoxville when I stopped at the Mercury Theater to see who would be playing there and when. What luck! I saw my friend Bing Fu whom I knew from his work at Moose's Music Hall and with the band Dreve. Bing was helping to promote this show and that's when I got introduced to Acid Bath as members and the band's crew were loading gear into the venue. The Mercury Theater closed a few years later, but in its days was well-known for hosting hardcore music acts.

84. Charles and Teresa Harris. Met in 1991.

I met Charles and his wife Teresa through my brother Robert's love for American Civil War history. Robert and my dad met the Harris' at a relics show in Marietta and soon became friends with them. Charles has authored books on relic hunting and has been featured on the TV show "Good Morning America" with Willard Scott. Charles has helped to excavate Lookout Mountain in Tennessee and Chickamauga Battlefield in Georgia. Teresa is well-known for her mastery of the art of wood carving. She carved the horses and animals on the famous carousel merry-go-round by the river in Chattanooga. We've been to their home and have seen their personal, private collections.

85. Torria Dora in Warner Robins at the pet crematorium 2004.

This was a great band whom I met at a show that was played to mostly high school kids at a local pet crematorium in Warner Robins, Georgia.

86. Gospel Hoe Down on Channel 3 in Spring of 2007.

My good Latino friends at Moivimiento Cristiano Communion in Dalton, Georgia have been on this show regularly for a few years. The musicians from Moivimiento play on this show and they invited me to go with them and share my testimony on the air. Cool show. I really enjoyed myself.

87. Jim "Thunder" Thornton in the Fall of 2000.

This guy was a billionaire who initially made his fortune in the carpet industry located in Dalton, Georgia. I was a senior at Tennessee Wesleyan College and some buds from the fraternity Sigma Phi Epsilon (SPE) invited me to go to a great party at Thunder's mansion. My friends wanted me to join and thought it was a great way to introduce me to everyone and help me decide. Thornton threw the party, because he is a graduate of Tennessee Wesleyan and it was his SPE frat buddies who helped him start a lucrative carpet business. It was incredible to hangout with Mr. Thornton and to tour his home. I liked the pool, the bowling alley, the golf course, and the helicopter with a landing pad. Thunder was a gracious host. Even better was how he was so modest and down-to-earth.

88. Jeff Coffin of the Flecktones with Uptown Bogarts. Fall of 2002.

I got assigned an article to do on this incredible saxophone player. I reviewed his CD "Go Round" and wrote a preview article for a show he played. When I arrived at the venue, I stopped and spoke with him while the opening band Uptown Bogarts was playing. He autographed my article and my CD and was very appreciative. His show is the best performance I've ever seen on saxophone. He blew everyone away when he played a solo on two saxes at the same time. The Uptown Bogarts were an excellent local funk band. I loved their cover of the theme song from the TV show "Sanford & Son" that they played at this show.

89. Paul Joseph of Broken Heart in 2007.

I met Paul Joseph at his church in Georgia after one of the other members of his church invited me to visit his church. I was introduced to Paul and his wife and told that he had won a Grammy Award and a Dove Award for his work as a Christian recording artist. I was told he used to play with the group Broken Heart. Paul was so cordial and friendly. He said he was friends with Future Man of Bela Fleck's band The Flecktones. I went once to one of the praise band practices at his church and jammed some with them. I didn't play trumpet very well that evening and I was pretty intimidated jamming with such high caliber musicians, but Paul and company told me not worry about it, said I did fine, and invited me to come back and jam with them. I had planned to do so, but then I met my lovely wife Katie, moved to Atlanta, and started jamming with her every day!

90. Went to Charleston, SC with Troop 448 in 1987 to stay on USS Yorktown.

My younger brother Robert and I went on this trip with our Boy Scout troop and stayed overnight at the USS Yorktown. We toured the city of Charleston and got to go to many famous and historical places including Fort Sumter where the American Civil War began. We went to Folly Beach which was later excavated by enthusiasts looking for relics. We didn't know at the time that we were playing on top of valuable artifacts. We were just having fun at the beach and going for a swim.

91. Mary Catherine the senator's daughter for Monster's Ball. Fall 2001.

I was assigned a review of the movie Monster's Ball. I asked my neighbor Mary Catherine to go with me. She was taller than me and played basketball. She said her father was a Senator, but he wasn't from Memphis like she was. I forget which state he represented. Anyhow, we were on a guest list for a special preview of Monster's Ball that was shown only to local members of the press before the film was released to the general public. There was wine and hors devours set out for guests. We had to present our passes upon arrival. I thought the movie had an excellent plot and I gave it an A rating in my review. However, I must note that I recommended the film for mature viewers due to the nudity and content in the film. That clause was edited out of the final edit of my article that went to print. Anyhow, Mary Catherine seemed to like the movie as well. I just thought it was cool to mention that I went to this special viewing for free AND with a senator's daughter. Like that made her more special or something... *smirk*

92. The Drifters for the Duncan Family BBQ. Fall of 2001.

I saw and heard The Drifters at the Duncan Family BBQ sing their famous classic "Under the Boardwalk." It was cool to see and hear them live. I was a guest for this event, because I worked with Congressman Jimmy Duncan's sister Becky at the Sertoma Center. She invited me because my grandparents (Hester) used to be neighbors and friends with her father the late Congressman John Duncan, Sr. I also met at this event former Tennessee Governor and Presidential candidate Lamar Alexander and Senator Bill Frist.

93. Elmer with Aaron and Sean, Fall of 1996.

My buds Aaron Armour and Sean Parrish booked this totally excellent band of "hillbilly punks" from Portland, Oregon named Elmer. The band was all so cordial and friendly. I remember the lead singer looked like actor Rob Sneider from Saturday Night Live. It was uncanny. Anyhow, after the show I told that singer his band's sound reminded me a lot of the band Green Day. That's when I learned Elmer was from Portland and had played several shows with Green Day prior to Billy Joe Armstrong and company having become mainstream favorites. The whole band crashed at my friends Aaron and Sean's apartment after the show. It was a funny seen with folks sleeping wherever they could catch a wink. Even more glamorous was the old schoolbus parked outside in the parking lot of this nice apartment community. We sat around munching on pizza while we watched our Jim Henson favorite "Emmet Otter's Junk Band Christmas." Ah, such sweet memories...

94. Holly Denman Book Release. May 3, 2003.

I had to mention this to readers! I met this incredible artist Holly Denman at an Elmer show in 1996. She did illustrations and drawings. I later saw her occasionally at UT when I was attending graduate school there. One evening I saw her at Starbucks and she invited me to her book release party. She did some excellent illustrations for James J. Molchan's book "Of Myth and Legend." Look for her work and support her!

95. John Scofield with Topaz. June 2002.

I think I wrote a preview article for this event, but I'm not sure. I went because I knew about John Scofield and had been put on a guest list for his show. I enjoyed his work with Miles Davis and what he did on Blue Note Records. Before the show I found a greatest hits CD of John Scofield and he graciously signed it when we met that evening. My friend J.C. Haun was there hanging out with me and he got him to sign an old acoustic guitar.

While listening to Topaz open, I was chatting with a representative from the excellent funk band's label Velour Records. She gave me Topaz's CD and it was phenomenal. I published a review article in the Daily Beacon Newspaper about Topaz' CD "The Zone." It received an A and is one of my favorite articles.

96. Saw Guns n' Roses with Skid Row. June 26, 1991.

Oh my gosh! I went to this "test fest" if you will. I went to this testosterone-drenched concert all alone, but I just HAD to be there. It's funny, because at the time I was obsessed with GNR. Slash was my "guitar hero" in those days and I wanted to have long hair and a hat just like his. I remember the tickets were expensive, even for the nosebleed section where I was sitting. The show was at Thompson Bowling Arena on the campus of the University of Tennessee in Knoxville. I later learned on a camping trip that my Boy Scout leader Harry Carroll worked as GNR's personal security that night after the show when they rented out a local movie theater, because Harry worked for the Knox County Sherriff's Department. The details of that story will stay with me and Harry...

97. Van Halen on tour with Baby Animals February 16, 1992.

I went with my brother Robert to see this legendary rock band in the winter of 1992. I remember standing in line with him in the cold for a couple of hours so we could get tickets for this sold-out show. I paid extra and got us the "Gold Circle Seats," so I could be close to Eddie Van Halen and watch his fingers shred. I really enjoyed sitting in the corner on the side Eddie was on. It was a great show and I got a good look at Eddie and his mates. Sammy Hagar led everyone in the classic "I Can't Drive 55." Baby animals were pretty cool and had a decent set, but I haven't heard their music since that show. They were a band from Australia. I've heard that they had a good fan base there.

98. Lee Greewood at Homecoming '86 Jamboree.

I went camping with my Boy Scout troop 448 in the fall of 1986 to this great gathering just outside of Nashville. Homecoming '86 celebrated Tennessee being 200 years old as an American state. Scouts gathered from all over Tennessee and from neighboring states. Lee Greenwood sang "God Bless the USA" and a few others tunes. It was the only time I have seen him perform live, but hopefully not the last.

99. Ozzy with Alice in Chains and Sepultura. October 25, 1992.

Yes! This was one of the greatest concerts I've ever been to! What an excellent memory. Brazilian thrash-metal greats Sepultura opened for this show. It was SO excellent. The machine-gun fire of guitar chords layered with

Max Cavelera's lead vocals and backed by Igor Cavelera pounding my senses on drums was great! I loved Sepultura! If they do a reunion and tour, I'll be there! I loved those guys and I still have some sheet music of their songs. My favorite song I remembered hearing was "Arise." After Sepultura pummeled listeners into submission, I had the treat of seeing one of rock's great legends sing in rare form. Alice in Chains' lead vocalist Layne Stayley rolled out on stage in a wheelchair with one of his legs in a fat, white, cast. The leg in a cast was propped up in the air and sticking out on a foot rest. Layne was wearing his signature black sunglasses. The brother took some crutches he was toting with him, got up out of the chair, and stood up with a crutch under each arm. He proceeded to sing an entire set while leaning on crutches! I crowd surfed for the first time at this show. My skinny little Caucasian body went atop the hands of the masses in a packed coliseum full of fans. It was sort of surreal for a few minutes as I surfed over in front of the stage and waved at Layne and guitarist Jerry Cantrell. The show was general admission and no seats were assigned. The floor in front of the stage was free and clear for standing. My bud Joe Greenwood and I stood there in front of the stage next to Jerry Cantrell. We got separated until the end of the show after I looked over and saw the "eye of the hurricane." With just as much force and fury that mosh pit was indeed brutal. I said to Joe "Hey look! Mosh pit! Let's go!" We went into that swirling frenzy of disorder and ultimately got separated until the end of the show. It was a "don't tell mom" event. There were two big guys beating the life out of each other in that pit. I have been told one was "strung out on coke." The guy who was lit kicked the teeth out of the other not-so-lucky guy. I tried to avoid the blood and the teeth flying by me. It took me at least ten minutes to get out of that pit, because folks in the crowd cold-heartedly kept pushing me back in! What a mess! What a rush! I did it! I was tough! I was mean! I was bad! I was STUPID! What was I thinking? I had just gotten out of an adolescent treatment unit. It wasn't too wise of me to take the risk that I did, but I suppose that's the nature of many healthy teenage boys. After successfully navigating my way out of the mosh pit, I was allowed to relax and take a breather. Good 'ol Ozzy was up next! His music wasn't "the mosh kind." Ozzy ran out on stage with a bucket of water and threw it on the crowd. I got hit by it! It had special powers! *grin* I drooled as I stood in front of guitarist Zaak Wylde. He played some great Ozzy classics including "No More Tears" and my favorite "Crazy Train." That Ozzy water must have had special powers, because I'm still riding the crazy train.

100. The Dead Milkmen at Flamingos. Fall of 1992.

I was all set, or so I thought, to meet this awesome indie band that I absolutely loved in my high school years (I still dig their music). Well, mom and I decided I should get some help for my adolescent path of self-destruction. I went into the hospital at Saint Mary's the week they were playing in Knoxville at Flamingos. I don't remember the exact date, but I know that I tried to postpone my rehab for this show. I was sure that I would have gotten to meet them at Flamingos. Or maybe not... I might not have been able to get someone to let me into the show, because Flamingo's usually required patrons to be at least 18. Hopefully I can see them later when they read this book.   *smile*

101. **Mardi Gras with Lynyrd Skynyrd March 12, 2005.**

It was completely by coincidence that I met the keyboardist Billy Powell and whoever was playing guitar with Skynyrd that night at Universal Studios Theme Park in Orlando. I don't know for sure who it was that played guitar that night since a few weeks earlier guitarist Hughie Thomasson left Skynyrd to reform the Outlaws. I talk briefly about this event in the last chapter of this book, so read on!

102. **Missed going to see Public Enemy in October 1992.**

As if going to see Ozzy, Alice in Chains, and Sepultura wasn't reward enough, I went out and purchased a ticket to my favorite "rhyme animals" Public Enemy. I didn't even ask my mom first, because I thought for sure I would be there. WRONG!!! That day will forever remain in infamy! *smirk* This show caught me and a lot of other folks by complete surprise, because P.E. were scheduled to play at the Bijou Theater in Knoxville, which is not a large venue. Further, the legendary group was on its way to a historic show as it was scheduled to cross genres and open for rockers U2 in Atlanta the next day after playing in Knoxville. Curses! (Just kidding Mom!) Why did I have to be SO bad as a teenager? I remember not being allowed to go because of my poor academic performance and my less than respectful attitude. I remember whining and complaining to my mom, but she was right. I was just an immature little snot and all I wanted to do was party and have a good time like most kids. Mom made me a promise I couldn't refuse. She would have called the cops on me if I had taken the car and gone to that show. This was definitely one of the many rock scars I earned in life.

103. **Jammed with Greg Stevens of Confederate Railroad. December 2006.**

One of my neighbors at the apartment community I lived in invited me to the place in Dalton called Fred's Music Hall. It was a small country music and rockabilly establishment. It was an all-ages venue. Anyhow, I brought my trumpet along and got to jam on some great classics including the song "Johnny Be Good" with the house band my first night. It was a great jam and everybody seemed to dig it, even though having a trumpet was quite unusual for folks at Fred's. Greg Stevens who used to play keyboards for Confederate Railroad was jamming on the keys with us. Greg also played some guitar for us and sang a little as well. It was a treat to meet him and everybody at Fred's my first time going in December. I was told he played there regularly. I visited a few more times in the weeks to follow, but stopped as trumpet just really didn't fit with the venue's music. It was a cool experience for me though.

104. Todd Steed and Apelife with Cracker and LP. Fall of 2002.

I went to this excellent show with my best bud Eric as a guest, because I was on assignment to write about Cracker and Apelife for The Daily Beacon Newspaper. I called Todd Steed, because he happened to be an admissions counselor at UT while I was already there as a graduate student. He played guitar for Apelife and he had opened for Camper Van Beethoven a few years prior, which was David Lowery of Cracker's old band. The Daily Beacon let me have this assignment, because I had already met Cracker a couple years prior and had written about them. Plus, I asked for it. I've got Cracker soul!

105. Went to Israel in July of 1999.

This was an incredible and deeply spiritual journey for me. I prayed about it a lot before I went, particularly because I didn't want to get blown up or held hostage. I had the opportunity to go to England, Russia, Costa Rica, or China also, but I chose to make this trip because at the time of my decision Israel was relatively peaceful and had not experienced violent attacks for some time. I wanted to see the land that was home to Abraham and to Christ. I earned religion course credit there through Hiwassee College where I had earned my associates degree. I went because I felt like it might be my last chance to visit before fighting started again and safety diminished. I was right. While out on tour one day there was thunder in the sky, but no rain. It was a bright and sunny day, plus it usually rained about once or twice a year in Israel then. I looked up and saw F-15 military jets flying through the sky at various times throughout the day. When I returned to The Seven Arches Hotel in Jerusalem that evening I learned that the thunder I heard was from some bombs that had exploded in neighboring Palestine. It saddens me that Israel and its neighbors have not coexisted with complete peace for thousands of years. While on this trip, I visited the Palestinian territories, parts of Gaza, the West Bank, the Dead Sea, the Mediterranean Sea, and stopped at a border checkpoint that Israel and Jordan shared. I actually looked over Jordan while leading my travel companions in the old hymn "Swing Low Sweet Chariot." I met many fine persons from Christian, Muslim, and Jewish faiths on this trip who helped educate me and share their perspectives on Israel and its neighbors.

106. Went to Nicaragua for missionary work. Summer 2004.

This was another deeply meaningful and spiritual journey for me. I went on this trip with a group from Faith Promise Church, my old church in Knoxville. I heard about the opportunity from my mom and I prayed about it. I went with a team to deliver mostly humanitarian aid. We had doctors, nurses, and dentists go with us in our group. We had cases of donated medicines and pharmaceutical items that we flew down with us to give out. At the time, the average Nicaraguan man earned only $500 a year (American money). However, Nicaragua and its people were beautiful. They were content with so much that Americans take for granted. I especially enjoyed visiting the volcanoes there and going to the beach on the west coast side of the country. I didn't bring my trumpet, but now wish I had because I loved the music I heard.

107. The Daily Beacon Newspaper fall of 2001 to Spring of 2002.

When I began my studies at the University of Tennessee, earning my master's degree was not my only ambition. I chose to accept opportunities and wrote for the school's newspaper while I was a student there. I wrote every semester I attended except my last because I was working a job full-time while doing my research full-time as a graduate student. Because of my acceptance into graduate school and my choosing to pursue a master's degree, I put my own personal magazine, The Vüe, on hold. I decided that I would write for the university's newspaper, so I could still meet people, make connections, and get people familiar with my work as a journalist. From the countless numbers of concerts and events that I experienced and wrote about, it looks like I made a wise choice.

108. Went on a mission trip with BSU to Charleston, SC Spring Break 1998.

It was Spring Break and I was a full-time student at Hiwassee College. I went the school's Baptist Student Union to Charleston to help folks in the inner-city areas by doing things such as painting on houses, neighborhood parties with children, and visiting local church youth to share my testimony. This was a good character-building experience for me. It helped me learn more not to be conceited and focused on myself as much as focused on helping others.

109. Fugazi. 2000.

I went to this show at The Electric Ballroom in Knoxville mainly because I loved the lead singer Ian McKay's work with his previous band, hardcore punk legends Minor Threat. It was a pretty good show, but there were some issues with crowd control and security. However, I still had a great time and got to see some of my best buds from Oak Ridge, Tennessee. I saw Robert

Childs and Matt Hall both at this show. I lost touch with those two. Maybe they'll get back in touch with me after seeing their names in this incredible literary accomplishment. *smile*

110. **National Boy Scout Jamboree August 2-8, 1989.**

As mentioned earlier in this book, I went to the National Boy Scout Jamboree in August of 1989. This event was held at Fort A.P. Hill, a military base in Virginia. I was the big, bad, super-cool, bugler who represented East Tennessee and all of Knoxville in my conceited teenage glory. I played, they heard! I was seen, I looked great! I let folks know when to wake or sleep, when to eat, or when to salute the flag! I tooted my own horn proudly. I talk about my ego earlier in this book. This event helped build my self-confidence, but I'm glad I lost the conceit.

111. **NFL Hall of Famer Gayle Sayers. Fall of 1999.**

Speaking of Boy Scouts, I am reminded of how I met this NFL great. There was a special fund-raiser banquet that I attended in Athens, Tennessee held in the cafeteria at Tennessee Wesleyan College. Chicago Bears great Gayle Sayers was the guest speaker and he shared about the good experiences he had as a Boy Scout. He encouraged everyone to support the program. I went because I was an Assistant Scoutmaster for Troop 114 in Englewood, Tennessee at that time. I spoke briefly with Gayle after the banquet and he signed my program. Cool!

112. **Incubus at Moose's Music Hall, Tim got hit on as Nick Cage. 2000.**

Heh...Heh... This is a funny memory, but a good one! The rock band Incubus was just starting to get popular and was promoting its CD "S.C.I.E.N.C.E." I think the band Ultraspank opened up for them. Anyhow, just as my youngest brother Tim Hester and I walked through the front door and into the venue, a young lady tried to make a move on Tim! Only she tried the WRONG pickup line with the Tim-meister! She made the mistake of telling Tim what countless others had told him before: "Hey! Has anybody ever told you that you look like a young Nicholas Cage?" Um... Not good little missy. STRIKE ONE! YOU'RE OUT!!! Tim just looked up at the ceiling, rolled his eyes, said "Gee, thanks." Anyhow, after pestering Tim about that girl, we made it upstairs and in front of the stage where we had a great view and listen of Incubus. The band played very well and little did we know that a short time later Incubus would become a huge commercial success. Little did those chicks know that my brother Tim was sick of hearing he looked like Nick Cage, even though he liked the man's acting. *grin*

113. **Lake Tahoe with buds Aaron Armour and Greg Kimmel. June 2003.**

This was my first time going out to California and the West Coast. I had a BLAST! I flew into Sacramento, California. Upon arrival, I got a rental car at the airport and drove it to Greg and Aaron's house in Lake Tahoe. Awesome ride and such beautiful country I remember. What a great adventure! Once I got to Tahoe, I settled in at Aaron and Greg's like we had never been apart for more than a day. I'm sure it will be that way next time I see them. They're both great guys and they are just SO funny! While there we went to lakes and beaches, went hiking, went to some casinos, and had some great food at local restaurants. We also went to Reno and to Carson City in Nevada. I put about 3,000 miles on my rental car in one week! Greg and I went out to San Francisco for a day so I could see the Golden Gate Bridge. I went there and also to a rocky, shark-infested piece of coastline, just so I could say I've been to the Pacific Ocean! While In Tahoe, I went to a great music store called Mad About Music. This was a great trip and a wonderful lifetime memory.

114. **Carey Archer of Mr. Skinny and AC Entertainment and his wife Erin.**

I met Carey Archer in 2000 when he was playing keyboards for a funk band called Mr. Skinny. He's a nice guy with a great talent on keys. I saw Mr. Skinny play a time or two live with my cousin Cyrus Lloyd, because he knew the band's lead singer and guitarist Davis. Mr. Skinny was a great band, but many folks including myself thought they needed some horns. My cousin Cyrus plays sax and he had been talking with them for some time. They gave us their demo CD and we practiced jamming on it for some time and had the horn parts worked out. Unfortunately, Mr. Skinny broke up before the world would have heard mine and and Cyrus' great horn work. *smirk* At some point, Carey married Erin Tipton the highly accomplished violinist from the band Jag Star whom I mentioned previously in this book. Last I heard, Carey was doing booking and promotions for AC Entertainment and his wife Erin was teaching private music lessons.

115. **Miles Davis Tribute at Blue Cats 10-24-01.**

I wrote a preview for this show which was at Blue Cats. It got published in the Daily Beacon. I'm sure it was great, but ultimately I was unable to go because I was wise enough to stay home and study for a test I had because I was in graduate school at UT. My friend J.C. Haun played guitar in it and was the one who originally told me about it. He still gave me a really cool t-shirt with a great black and white photo of Miles Davis on the front and thanked me for my support.

116. **Roosevelt Center at Warm Springs in March 2005.**

I went to this excellent rehabilitation facility for training in Warm Springs, Georgia when I was a vocational rehabilitation counselor for the Georgia Department of Labor. It was the place President Franklin Roosevelt stayed to get rehabilitated when he battled having polio. As when President Roosevelt had stayed there so long ago, Warm Springs was still a quiet small town. I thoroughly enjoyed my stay there. I remember some other trainees and myself entertained ourselves at a local karaoke bar. I did a blistering rendition of Steppenwolf's classic "Born to Be Wild." I stood up on a bar stool, crawled across the floor, and had the place raving buck wild. It was great! I sang that song the way Ian Astbury of The Cult did when they played that song. While there at Warm Springs, I learned that the band Slipknot would be playing in Atlanta a few days later on its "Subliminal Verses Tour." Naturally, I got a ticket and went, because I am and always will be the rock star of rehab!

117. **Everlast Fall of 2000.**

Oh my gosh! This was an excellent show. If memory serves me correctly, there wasn't even an opening band, so Everlast played extra long. My cousin Cyrus went with me and he drove. We arrived at the Electric Ballroom and found radio jockeys Mancow, Freak, and Turd opening the event with their usual, crass, sick humor. Everlast played all of his current hits from the album "Whitey Ford Sings the Blues." He also got things hopping when he played an excellent rendition of his former group House of Pain's smash "Jump Around." After enjoying a few hours of good jams, Cyrus and I left the club in the wee hours to go get some coffee and head for home. We got about two blocks from the venue and we noticed a young lady walking up the hill in the cold while we were sitting at a traffic light. Cyrus said "She doesn't need to be walking out there in the cold at this time of night. I'm gonna see if she wants a ride." Where we were at was not the safest part of Knox Vegas, particularly at that time of night. So, naturally Captain Rehab and Saint Cyrus sprang into action! Cyrus rolled the window down and asked the girl "Hey, you look cold. Want to get some coffee with us at the convenient store there on the corner?" The poor girl was trashed. She got in the car and we road across the street to get coffee. Cyrus went in and got the coffee for all of us while the inebriated lass sat wearily in the back seat telling me her life's story. Apparently, the guy the girl had gone to the concert with was an obnoxious wretch. He left the show irate with some other girl. So, the young woman Cyrus and I rescued was left alone without a ride home. After Cyrus got back in the car she agreed to let us drive her home. She lived across town, but thankfully it was in the direction we were headed. Cyrus and I are pretty streetwise, so we didn't want this girl's number or anything else to do with her after that night. We drove her to some apartments where she said her car was. She found her car, but Cyrus and I refused to let her drive and insisted on her waiting for a friend. After knocking on a friend's apartment door numerous times and waiting about ten minutes, another girl opened the door. Our intoxicated friend explained what happened and we made sure that jerk guy wasn't around and Cyrus and I said our goodbyes. This is just one example of sad reality in the many I have experienced when traveling along the rock 'n roll highway.

118. **Charlie Daniels with Wynona Judd in Atlanta. May 23, 2004.**

This was originally when I was supposed to meet Charlie Daniels. As mentioned earlier in this writing, my friend got sick and was not able to go with me to this show. Because the tickets and guest list passes were in her name, the Hi-Fi Buys will-call station would not let me have the backstage pass, but only gave me the ticket and special VIP seating. Oh well, no biggie. It was a great show!

119. **Knoxville Museum of Art –Escher Exhibit in 2000.**

I love M.C. Escher! The man was a genius! I went with Professor Julie Jack-Warren to this exhibit as a field trip with my classmates from Tennessee Wesleyan College. Some of Escher's original works were at the Knoxville Museum of Art. They even had some original wood cuts and metal plates he used to make prints with. I highly recommend this guy's artwork to anyone!

120. **Spoke at Convocations at TWC and played trumpet in 2001.**

Looking back on this event I feel like a jerk. Tennessee Wesleyan College students were required to attend convocation, or church services on campus. I shared some at a TWC convocation, but like Hiwassee College, I just wanted people to notice me and how much I had accomplished in spite of my disability. I played my trumpet once at a convocation and it was very mediocre. I learned later on that my old horn was leaking some air and that because of the leak I had to blow harder and overcompensate for the leak. When I got the leak fixed and the horn cleaned out, wow! I was a stronger player. Okay, so I'm making an excuse as to why my playing was yucky. I played an old song by Michael W. Smith along with the college's Music instructor who was playing the pipe organ. Anyhow, I was REALLY nervous playing in front of the whole college and all of the many academic minds in church at TWC. I just hope that some of what I said and did helped draw someone closer to God.

121. **Sang in choir with Methodist Church in Dallas –2000.**

I went to a conference in the Fall of 2000 in Dallas, Texas that was at the Hilton Hotel of the Dallas / Ft. Worth Airport. It was a conference for high school and college students considering ordained ministry. I went with a group of students from the Holston Conference of the United Methodist Church. I sang Baritone in a large choir made up of other students from all over America. I road in a private chartered tour bus all the way from Knoxville, Tennessee to Dallas, Texas. So, rock stars and celebrities traveling often on the road have my complete sympathy! I never did go to seminary and become ordained, but I still enjoyed the fellowship at this event.

122. **Won Morton Award in 1998.**

Wow! What a pleasant surprise this was to me! The English Department at Hiwassee College was so good to me. It's because of Hiwasse College that I am a writer now. Dr. Curtis Chapman and Dr. Jim Schiavoni especially encouraged me and helped me to express myself through writing. I found out at the end of the year in a special assembly that I was awarded the Morton Award for writing poetry because of some of the poems I submitted to the college's literary magazine.

123. **Was in the play "You Can't Take it with You." Fall 1998.**

This play was so much fun. It's a great comedy classic. I am so glad that I got to be a part of a few productions presented on campus at Hiwassee College. I had a small supporting role as a government agent. However, even that part took a lot of time and practice. It was cool to wear a trench coat and a top hat and talk in such a gruff tone. I especially appreciate all that I learned about theater under the guidance and direction of Edward Powers. Thanks Eddie!

124. **Saw Gran Torino play its last show. Fall 2001.**

I went to this event with my cousin Cyrus Lloyd and my best bud Eric -you guessed it- Davis. Gran Torino were and still are my favorite funk band of all time. There was just SO much talent assembled together in this group that it was a sad day for me to see Gran Torino come to an end. I heard that the group's manager Ted Heinig merged his company with Ashley Capps' AC Entertainment and moved from Knoxville to Nashville. This band was a huge influence on my writing and on my trumpet playing. I wish them all the best.

125. **Stayed at the Foundry Inn and met Dixie Dirt. July 2005.**

I had some training that I was required to go to with my good friend Mike Avant when we worked together for The Georgia Department of Labor as vocational rehabilitation counselors. The training took place at the Foundry Inn of Athens, Georgia in July of 2005. Mike and I shared a room together there at the inn. While there, we visited a really great art museum next door which had original pieces for album covers of the bands Days of the New and R.E.M. There was a lot of excellent artwork in that gallery. I was thumbing through a local paper one evening after training and found a listing for a band from Knoxville called Dixie Dirt who would be playing at the world famous 40 Watt Club in Athens. Mike and I went out for the show and to my pleasant surprise I knew the band's manager Lenore Kinder who was with them. She used to manage Blue Cats for awhile and had worked in promotions for Workhorse Management. She has also worked for the Bonnaroo Festival. Anyhow, it was great to see her again after a few years. Mike and I sat around and chatted with Dixie Dirt who shared with us many insights about the music industry including an offer they had received from MTV. Dixie Dirt played an excellent show that evening. They went on to become performers at Bonnaroo a short time later.

126. **Interviewed Cookie Cutter Girl. Summer 2008.**

I interviewed Lynn Julian a.k.a. Cookie Cutter Girl for Target Audience Magazine. She a great artist with a lot of enthusiasm. She has done a lot to support indie artists and musicians. Read the article I wrote in the previous chapter of this book! If you've already read it, do it again!

127. **Reviewed the LB Collective CD.**

This Atlanta-based group's lead singer and namesake of the band Laura Benjamin personally mailed me a promo package with a note and a CD. I really enjoyed her CD and the review can be found in the previous chapter of this book. Read it!

128. **Ministry interview on April 25, 2008.**

As stated previously in this book, Ministry was one of my favorite bands in my high skull days and getting to meet them and write about them was a treat. I still dig Al Jourgensen's music and in the course of writing this book I learned shortly after interviewing some of Ministry's members that the group received its fifth nomination for a Grammy Award. Read that interview in this book!

129. **The Inauguration of President Barack Obama. 1-20-09.**

I worked at a local elementary school today as a substitute teacher all day with a class of excellent second grade students. We watched the inauguration of America's first African-American President. I have things that I disagree with Obama on and with McCain on, but there are also things I agree with both on. Hopefully, readers can appreciate the fact that America values diversity and will judge candidates on their abilities and the "contents of their characters," rather than the color of their skin or their political affiliations.

130. **5-2-08   Was supposed to interview Cracker this evening in Atlanta.**

Showed up to the venue and for whatever reason I was not on the guest list. Katie and I were disappointed, because she had never heard Cracker live before. So, we made a night of it anyways. We hung out in the "Little Five Points" section of Atlanta around Moreland Avenue. Katie and I walked around and at one point noticed we were being stalked by a street thug, so we jetted into a record store. We went to a cool shop across the street from Performer Magazine's office. The groovy little music store was called *Criminal Records.*

131. **Saturday 5-3-08 Camping with Katie's Dad:**

Katie and I woke up bright and early this morning at 6:00, so we could drive to a campground near Asheville, North Carolina and spend a couple of days with Katie's dad, her step-mom, her uncle and his wife. It was really nice and located in a quiet, remote area. It had trails, a lake, and a waterfall. We drove through the dusty redneck roads of South Carolina to get there and back. They were "Cadillac camping" in nice RV trailers they pulled behind their pickup trucks.

132. **Dreve and Alpha Zulu. Fall 2000.**

I don't remember the name of the club that this show was at, but my friend Joseph came with me. Dreve had just announced that they had been signed by Atlantic Records and were celebrating with this show. Dreve was Brent Smith of Shinedown's previous band. They played an incredible show with covers including "Hang Around" by Sugar Ray and "Ain't Goin' Out Like That" by Cypress Hill. I did a little bit of crowd surfing at this event and have a bad photo somewhere of me coming down off of the stage backwards onto the crowd. Yeah, I know. It was stupid, but it was fun. It was ROCK 'N ROLL!!! Alpha Zulu played a great set as well. An interesting fact is that my buddy Joesph who was a student at Wesleyan at the time did some acting when he was a kid on the Disney TV show "Kids Incorporated." It's a small world after all...

133. **August 31, 2001.   Grand Foot Ball at Blue Cats.**

I attended this event for the very first article I wrote for The Daily Beacon Newspaper. I wrote about my favorite Southern rock band Left Foot Down and this grand commemoration to celebrate the opening of Blue Cats and all college students returning to school for the fall. I wrote a preview article. The place was packed to capacity and as a guest I received V.I.P. treatment. Guitarist John Montgomery of Left Foot Down appreciated my article and gave me a cool t-shirt specially made for that event. I still have that shirt!

134. **Received the July 2008 issue of Performer 7-25-08. Jammed at Covenant of Peace in Woodstock, Georgia.**

Ellen Eldridge has some of her work in the current issue of Performer. She does writing and photography. She's a longtime friend of my wife Katie and is also the owner and Editor in Chief of Target Audience Magazine, so that makes her my friend too! Katie and I played at Covenant of Peace tonight with members of Invitation. We had a blast! It was what Covenant of Peace called "Cafe' Night." It was an open-mic session for local artists to express their praises to God. There were also paintings and drawings on display from local artists as well. Cool gig.

135. **Bad Email!!! August 7, 2008.**

Learned today after checking my email that my favorite place to hear live music, the Serene Bean will be closing this coming Saturday.

136. **Katie and I went to the Serene Bean for its last night open.**

It was August 9, 2008. I remember it well. The favorite spot for local artists, Serene Bean, officially closed after that evening. The place where my wife and I had enjoyed sharing some tunes and poetry with locals closed. We had our last espressos and pumpkin muffins, signed the guest book, and said goodbye to a great venue. The host of the open-mic, Dale Capri, promised folks he would continue his support of local artists by hosting open-mic events at other establishments. Thanks for the sweet memories Serene Bean. Thanks for all of the great jams Dale.

137. **Met The Strength Coach. March 2005.**

I love this guy! Greg "The Strength Coach" Smith is the best! I enjoyed his clever conversation and his enthusiasm laced with tons of humor. We met at the National Rehabilitation Association's annual conference in March of 2005. The event was held at The Embassy Suites Hotel at Bush Gardens in Tampa, Florida. It was a conference for professional counselors and rehabilitation professionals. I was working at that time as a Vocational Rehabilitation Counselor for the Georgia Department of Labor. Greg was a motivational speaker and a syndicated radio DJ. He is the author of "On a Roll." It is a great inspirational book about overcoming one's adversities. Buy this dude's book! This event reminded me of how like most "professional" conferences certain things are done to entertain attendees. I remember that besides the speeches and seminars there were drinks, hors devours, and door prizes given away. There was even a nice dance with a DJ one evening for all of the rehabilitation professionals who actually wanted to "get jiggy." This event is just one example of the many professional events that I have attended where there was always some form of entertainment. That's why I'm affectionately known by my peers as "the rock star of rehab." *smirk*

138. **August 19, 2008. Went to Christian Songwriters in Marietta.**

My wife Katie and I heard about this group of songwriters from our good friend Ollie Patterson at our church. Ollie's an incredibly talented musician. He is especially great at playing saxophone and at playing guitar. Before he came to play music at Covenant of Peace Ministries (my church at the time this book was being finished), he wrote, arranged, and played music at Lakewood Church in Texas when Joel Osteen's father was the pastor. Katie and I played our song "Resurrect" this evening for the group's organizer Kate Thompson. She said she has written songs for and worked with numerous famous artists including Reba McIntyre and Casting Crowns. She's from Australia and has a cool accent. My wife and I were impressed with her heart for helping children as she has adopted many and has a large home for them.

139. **August 20, 2008 got an email from Kate Thompson.**

My wife Katie received an email today from Kate Thompson. She liked our song "Resurrect" and felt that we had a special anointing to play. She graciously has offered to give us a day in a recording studio near Atlanta with acclaimed producer John Johnson! Praise the Lord! Free studio time with a great producer!

140. **September 4, 2008 recording five songs with John Johnson.**

What a great time we had in the studio today! We had so much fun with John and he was so good to work with. We got five songs recorded. On the way to the studio I phoned and spoke to Debra Shepherd of the gospel music group The Shepherds and asked her to pray for Katie and I. We left a CD of The Shepherds for John Johnson to listen to. As mentioned earlier in this book, I used to go to church with the Shepherds and I played some trumpet with them at church.

141. **Jammed with Katie and Frank French at songwriters night 12-9-07.**

This is such a cool memory. I was still dating Katie at the time and she was active as a member of the Cherokee County Music Society here in Georgia. Well, they had a sort of open-mic kind of night at a local pub in Woodstock, Georgia to promote local artists and members of the music society. Katie played some of her own originals by herself singing and playing guitar. Later on that night, Katie and I got together with a group of other local musicians and jammed some great classic blues and Southern rock. On bass guitar we had Frank French who has worked extensively with the Indigo Girls as their producer! The two songs I remembered playing that I enjoyed the most were "Johnny Be Good" by Otis Redding and "Can't You See" by the Marshall Tucker Band. Katie was incredible and I was SO proud of her work as a flautist on that Marshall Tucker classic.

142. Met Joni Erickson Tada Fall 2002.

I met this incredible and inspirational lady one evening when she came as a guest speaker for one of the Assistive Technologies classes when I was in graduate school at UT. She is a renown advocate for persons with disabilities and is an incredible artist and radio program hostess.

143. Met the owner of Ziggy's in Winston Salem. April 2005.

My often-mentioned best friend Eric Davis took me to Ziggy's when I was visiting him back when he lived in Mebane, North Carolina. Eric somehow knew the owner of Ziggy's and he introduced me to him. We both loved Cracker and heard they were going to be at Ziggy's playing with Camper Van Beethoven whom we also liked a lot. I had a cold at the time and I talk some about this show and my hanging out with David Lowery of Cracker, because I had a bad cold that night. My favorite song of the evening was "Hippie Chicks" by Camper Van Beethoven, but it was all great. Even better was the smallness and intimacy of this renown music club.

144. Reviewed the Mule Thieves CD. Fall 2008.

I wrote a review of this great band from Athens, Georgia for Performer Magazine. The band's CD was well-produced and included a variety of styles. If they can keep things together, I predict that the Mules Thieves will succeed in their endeavors.

145. Reviewed the Dropsonic CD. Spring 2008.

Here's a good band from Atlanta that had an interesting sound. I don't want to label them, because they were very good. They reminded me some of The Rolling Stones and Jack White's stuff. I had a review of them published in the Southeast edition of Performer Magazine. I had a statement that I wrote in that review which might have been misinterpreted. Just for the record, I praised this band for its talent and it's ability, not for its use of the notorious f-word at the end of the CD I reviewed. Rock on!

146. Reviewed The Autumn Offering CD. Fall 2007.

Oh my gosh! I love this CD. I published a review in Southeast Performer about this excellent band hailing from Jacksonville, Florida. I think they are one of the better groups to come out of Jacksonville. Read the review here in this book also. I hope this great indie band has some success like so many others who've come out of Jacksonville.

147. Attended the Atlantis Music Conference with Katie on 9-20-08.

My wife Katie and I attended this excellent music conference on assignment from our friend Ellen Eldridge for her magazine Target Audience.

While at the conference, I interviewed producer Isaac "Ike Dirty" Hayes, III. We also met Grammy-winner Kendrick "Wylde Card" Dean, Grammy-winner Adonis Shropshire, Sonic Bids CEO Angela, and Denocka Wardrick of YouTube Raps. Cool event to help promote music.

148. Skillet backstage in Knoxville on February 28, 2000.

I went to the Knoxville Christian Center and got to hear and meet the excellent hard rock band Skillet. I still have the ticket, but the date is not printed on it. However the band's members signed it for me. I remember looking for a restroom and the band's incredible keyboard player helped me out. She stopped to help me and said I could the band's restroom in their dressing room. SWEET! I got to meet all of them. This was prior to the band getting signed by Atlantic Records and becoming a commercial success. They were all so cordial and friendly. They later did some shows with label mates Shinedown too!

149. Cross Seekers Convention in New Orleans 1998.

I attended this excellent conference with the Baptist Student Union of Hiwassee College. It was the first time I had been to New Orleans. We went to the River Walk and had some great Cajun food while we were there. At the Cross Seekers Conference I was treated to live performances from Steven Curtis Chapman, Anointed, Jars of Clay, and others. I had a lot of fun going on this trip. While there, my group and I went to the French Quarter one day and had a great lunch there. It was cool to get to see Bourbon Street.

150. Went to see 311 with the Roots in Atlanta at Lakewood. July 31, 2004.

I went to this show at Hi-Fi Buys, or Lakewood, in Atlanta. It was packed! My friend Toni came down from Knoxville with her boyfriend and met me there. There was so much smoke at this show, but the music was great! I enjoyed hanging out and watching these very influential artists in the VIP area under the canopy in front of the stage. "Jack-O-Lantern Weather" is one of my favorites by 311 and I actually play licks from it on my trumpet quite often. This show was funky and mellow. Cool.

151. Published a review of LP's CD in Fall 2002.

I met this kind little Italian lady when she was touring with Cracker. She was from New York. She gave me a copy of her CD and asked me to review it. I did so and gave it a great rating. I published a review for everyone at the University of Tennessee in the Daily Beacon Newspaper. I hope she is doing well and is still performing.

152. **Trans Siberian Orchestra in Atlanta with Katie November 16, 2008.**

Wow! Double wow! I knew that my wife Katie had already seen TSO twice and that this was one of her favorite groups of musicians, so I surprised her with tickets a few days earlier on her birthday. Katie is a classically-trained flautist. She has played flute with many orchestras. When she told me that members of two of my favorite metal bands, Savatage and Testament, played in this orchestra I knew I would enjoy seeing them with her. It blew my mind and I was completely impressed by my wife's knowledge of the Savatage classic "Hall of the Mountain King." It has always been one of my favorite guitar pieces. Anyhow, as you can see from this book, I've been to thousands of concerts and shows through the years. So, for me to say that this was the best rock concert I've ever been to is quite a statement. The musicianship was second to none. The whole event was impressive. The narrator was cool. The laser lights were excellent. However, I was SO impressed by the pyrotechnic work. Even the flames shot up to the beat of the music and changed colors according to different beats and sections of the songs. The ticket price for this show was a modest $20, plus service fees. Lastly, members of the orchestra impressed die-hard fans like myself by sticking around after the show to shake hands with fans and sign autographs! THERE IS A GOD IN HEAVEN! My wife and I got in line and all of the members of the orchestra signed our tickets, plus gave us some novelty TSO guitar picks. They were all so friendly. I almost fainted when I got some contact info from the group and Alex Skolnik told me to come check out his jazz band soon in Atlanta as well. I'M NOT WORTHY!!! I'M NOT WORTHY!!!

153. **December 7, 2008. Newsong Christmas Tour Celebration.**

My wife Katie and I went to a great concert this evening at the First Baptist Church of Woodstock, Georgia. Its pastor is Dr. Johnny Hunt. He is the President of the Southern Baptist Convention. Anyhow, the music was great this evening. Newsong, Rush of Fools, Ayiesha Woods, and American Idol Finalist Chris Sligh all performed very well. Katie and I met several of these musicians after the concert and got their autographs. Also just as a special note, I asked Reverend Hunt a personal question after the concert and I appreciate the very open and honest response he gave me that I promised not to publish.

154. **December 21, 2008. Christmas Music at Covenant of Peace Ministries:**

My wife and I had a great time playing Christmas music at church today. I played a trumpet solo with her on piano for the song "O Come Emmanuel." I also played a little bit of jazz and upon worship leader Ollie Patterson's prompting I played a little solo on one of the worship team's jams. We had a great dinner afterwards and celebrated with church family and friends. Katie and I also took some photos afterwards. The service was also recorded on CD. Cool. Happy Birthday Jesus!

Well, there are about a billion other wonderful "rock star events" that I could mention in this book, but these are just a few that will hopefully give readers a better idea of what average days are like in the incredible life of a rock 'n roll legend such as myself. I didn't have the time (or the energy) to write about every single event of my incredibly interesting and spectacular life (*smirk*), but after reading this catharsis of my absolute brilliance (indeed), hopefully readers have a better idea of why I have met just about any sort of person you can imagine. As Johnny Cash famously sang, "I've been everywhere man."

CHAPTER FIVE

Photo Gallery

My darling rock star wife and myself looking rather vogue! Give us your money!
Photo by Maduka Chidebelu-Eze.

Here's a shot of me hanging out with one of my favorite performers, country and gospel music legend Mr. Charlie Daniels, prior to his performance in Perry, GA. The photo was taken by his manager.

No, I am not Edward Norton! Folks seemed to dig this photo when I had it on MySpace. I swear, this unshaved look, has helped me meet several people that I wish I hadn't. Gee, thanks Edward. *grin* The photo was taken by my grandmother Mary Hester.

My cousin Cyrus Lloyd (middle) and I seen here with one of our favorite guitarists Johnny Hickman of the undeniably great Virgin recording artists Cracker! I was a guest for this show as a journalist writing about it. The photo was taken by my best bud Eric Davis.

Flying from the inside with my friend Brent Smith of Shinedown. We were at the Coca Cola Roxy Theater in Atlanta . I met the other bands Silvertide and Future Leaders of the World after our interview. Photo by Andrea Ashby.

Here I am with John Bechdel and Burton C. Bell of legendary industrial metal rock band Ministry after our interview in Atlanta. Ellen Eldridge is standing beside John. She's the Editor in Chief of Target Audience Magazine. Burton is standing beside me. Our interview was before Ministry's last show in Atlanta as a band. Ministry was on its last world tour in 2008. The photo was by Russell Eldridge.

Getting infected with Anthrax lead guitarist Rob Caggiano after my good friends shadowWax and Straight Line Stitch of Knoxville opened for Anthrax. He did an excellent job on lead, with John Bush singing, before the reunion of the longest lasting Anthrax lineup with Joey Belladona singing. After the reunion, Rob returned to the band full-time as the lead guitarist. Photo by my uncle David Hester.

Hanging out with bassist Kerry Morris and Three Dog Night's Drummer Pat Bautz after I played trumpet with them on a song at Cocoa Beach in Florida. This photo was snapped on the auto setting of my camera.

Here I am with Greg "The Strength Coach" Smith at a conference in Tampa, Florida. He's a syndicated radio DJ and is the author of the book "On a Roll." He's an incredible motivational speaker and a super guy. Look for his book and give him a listen! Photo by Dr. Lee Ann Rawlins.

Seen here with Tony Coelho at a dinner. He was the primary author of the Americans with Disabilities Act, a powerful piece of civil rights legislation. He ran Al Gore's Presidential Campaign in 2004. Tony was a US Congressman in California, and before that he worked for legendary comedian Bob Hope. Mr. Coelho was the President of the Epilepsy Foundation of America when we met, and also on CNN's Crossfire. He graciously tried to help me find a job, prior to my moving to Georgia. This photo was taken by Dr. Amy L. Skinner.

This is how rock stars sometimes feel after being holed up in a recording studio all day working on tracks non-stop for hours! Your tireless and dedicated producer, such as John Johnson seen here, can become the innocent victim of a crazed rock star's artistic passions! This photo was snapped by my lifeline, Mrs. Katie Hester.

Just a couple of cool cats hanging out after our Christmas concert in 2008.
Ollie Patterson is a great sax player and composer. He's the President of
Atmosphere. This photo was snapped by our friend Maduka Chidebelu-Eze.

Feeling a kindred spirit of rock 'n roll with guitarist Rocky Norman of the band
shadowWax just before the band opened for Sick Puppies in Knoxville. He's a
great guitarist! shadowWax like myself is from East Tennessee. The photo is by
my uncle David Hester.

This here is a photo of my favorite gansta ride! It took me to many places during the writing of this book and helped me meet many interesting people. It's been a part of the Hester family for 15 years. First it was my brother Tim's and then it was mine. I love this old car! In 2008, I sold it to my uncle David. I took this photo.

CHAPTER SIX

Tragedy is Entertainment

Tragedy as a form of entertainment is not something necessarily contemporary. For thousands of years, even before recorded history, humankind has been fascinated by watching others suffer. Many people have entertained thoughts of tragedy, and often they have acted upon them. Take for example the Roman Empire. During its reign, coliseums often filled with spectators watching two men (usually gladiators) battle against each other until one was left dead. This was often sport used to amuse the Caesar and his guests. At other times, people were placed in the center of an arena and made to fight starved animals such as lions, wolves, and tigers. The question of whether or not such entertainment is a tragedy, obviously is a matter of opinion. With that said, it is the assertion of this writer that such crude and inhumane forms of entertainment are tragedies, but even more tragic, perhaps, is that countless people found such to be perfectly acceptable.

Take, for example, the war in Iraq. I remember it starting under the administration of President George Bush, Senior while I was in 8th grade. Network TV and the media went on a frenzy covering this military, and political, objective. I remember watching the evening news and viewing images videoed with night-vision lenses that made everything look an emerald green. Or was it money green? Anyhow, it looked like stuff from the old sci-fi TV show *Battlestar Galactica*. The Topps company even printed up and sold "Desert Storm Trading Cards." In the collection of cards were photos of generals, military equipment, and the like. I remember seeing them at a local supermarket and thinking to myself "How sick and twisted is that?"

The freakin' war in Iraq and the "war on terror" is still being fought at the time of this writing. Not a day goes by without TV news, and other forms of media, entertaining the public by satisfying its hunger for tragedy. The masses buffet daily on juicy, sensationalized, coverage of a dysfunctional Iraq. So, why don't the major TV networks expose and televise the violence, and death it brings, in poor American communities nationwide? I guess they don't think it will sell for us to hear about the wars between gangs and factions in our own American ghettos, as well as it would to hear about it "happening over there." There is a bias in

American media that is very obvious to me, but I'll reserve my comments on that subject for a place other than this book.

In my opinion, American media's spotlight on death, scandal, and negativity is a tragedy. Just watch the daily news on TV, if you have the stomach for it. Images of a world full of violence and chaos seers the minds of viewers. It's no wonder that most teens seldom watch the news reported on TV. It's insensitive and depressing, mostly. It inspired the Seattle rock band *L7* to write the anthem "Wargasm," a cynical song about war, and how folks can be brainwashed, or at least desensitized, to the point of where watching images of war, and discussion of the subject, can become entertaining. It's like watching a scary movie. One's heart starts beating rapidly at the suspense of wondering what you will see and hear next.

I remember, as if it were yesterday, when I watched the video footage of the public execution of former Iraqi dictator Saddaam Hussein. The Iraqi leader having been found guilty for the murders of thousands, along with crimes against humanity, was hanged in a traditional manner with a rope around his neck at public gallows. I remember being at my friend Gary's apartment with him and his family. Discussion of the matter was on a TV news program. That program aired video footage of Saddaam's execution. It showed the trapdoor falling and suddenly Saddaam hanging from the rope around his neck while he squirmed. Not to pick on Gary's family, but when the trapdoor fell his mom, uncle, and other family and friends present were all cheering, with one yelling "He got what he deserved!" Gary gleefully yelled "Hey! Wait a minute! They didn't show it, they blocked it out."

I followed Gary into his bedroom where he had the unedited and uncensored video of Saddaam's death on his computer via the Internet. It was quite a scene. Everybody in the house was being entertained by watching a man die. Even though he might have deserved the execution he got, I still did not receive any pleasure in watching him die. However, the carnal part of my human psyche had its curiosity satisfied as I watched Saddaam die.

Don't misunderstand me. Based on the reported evidence I heard, Hussein's execution was justified, and I do support the death penalty when guilt has been established beyond any reasonable doubt. I just think it was sad to watch a man bitterly go to his death with no remorse for what he had been found guilty of. Prior to his death, I watched some of Hussein's court trial before his sentencing. Again, the trial and Saddaam shaking his fist and yelling at the judge were to me sick forms of public entertainment, as the spectacle was broadcast worldwide on television.

To be completely honest, my brothers and I played "war" a lot of the time when we were kids. We enjoyed role-playing the hunter and survivor roles we often saw portrayed on television. Our favorite vigilante gun slingers during childhood and in teenage years included *The Lone Ranger, Rambo, The Terminator, The Punisher, Dirty Harry, Batman,* and countless others. I mean, when I was a kid, my younger brothers and I had our little minds saturated with violence constantly. We either saw it on "free TV" or we watched movies on cable television. I mean who can forget every American boy's must-see cartoon *G.I. Joe*?

We watched the good guys every afternoon, after school, on Channel 43 conduct an onslaught against Cobra and his assemblies of villains. We would do some extreme stuff such as strapping our little action figures to bottle rockets or blowing up toy vehicles with cherry bombs. When we were little, my brother Robert and I would become cowboys on many an afternoon as he would dress up in his official *Lone Ranger* attire. He had the white cowboy hat, the black mask, the boots, the bandanna, and of course the silver six-shooters.

Countless studies have been conducted, and numerous observances have been made, regarding humanity's thirst to be entertained by violence. Maybe I sound like some kind of tree-hugging pacifist, but I think it is a bit tragic that the entertainment industry often focuses on and markets extremely violent and aggressive behaviors. Perhaps, that has contributed to the world currently being involved in a "war on terror." How could I ever forget watching old reruns of *Gunsmoke* or *Bonanza* with my dad? Such a wholesome way of living it was in America's "old West." If anyone or anything crossed ya, you wasted 'em.

Like a quote from the newscaster (couldn't find his name in the credits) who did a cameo appearance in the movie *Hot Shots*, he whimsically stared into the camera and said "War…It's Fan-Tastic!" --a spoof on the popular NBA commercial. In that same movie were spoofs making fun of Iraqi dictator Saddaam Hussein. Okay, I admit the movie Hot Shots is very funny, but it just alarms me how such a thing as war, can be used as entertainment. Other examples include the old TV shows *Mash* and *Hogan's Heros*. The show Mash was a lighthearted drama about the war in Vietnam. Whereas the latter was a comedy making fun of Hitler and the Nazis. I suppose that from a psychological perspective, entertainment can actually be used as a tool to help people face and cope with many of the world's concerns. I feel comfortable making that statement given the fact that I earned a master's degree in counseling, and I have worked in the counseling and human service fields for years.

A popular form of American entertainment that has had ample amounts of tragedy in the last two decades is WWE wrestling. Former wrestling star Marcus "Buff" Bagwell concurred when we met in 2008. He said the sport was often a very difficult and taxing profession. The program featuring mostly muscular stunt-men with acting skills has been heavily affected by the recent tragic deaths of many of its alumni. I found on the website about.com an article by Eric Cohen titled "*Wrestling's Dirty Secret.*" It contained a list of popular wrestlers, many of whom I loved to watch as a kid, who since 1985 died before the age of 65.

Names on the list include:

Chris Von Erich - 21
Mike Von Erich - 23
Louie Spiccoli - 27
Art Barr - 28
Gino Hernandez - 29
Jay Youngblood - 30
Rick McGraw - 30
Joey Marella - 30
Ed Gatner - 31
Buzz Sawyer - 32
Crash Holly - 32
Kerry Von Erich - 33
D.J. Peterson - 33
Eddie Gilbert - 33
The Renegade - 33
Owen Hart - 33
Chris Candido - 33
Adrian Adonis - 34
Gary Albright – 34
Bobby Duncum Jr. - 34
Yokozuna - 34
Big Dick Dudley - 34
Brian Pillman - 35
Marianna Komlos - 35
Pitbull #2 - 36
The Wall/Malice - 36
Leroy Brown – 38
Mark Curtis – 38

Eddie Guerrero - 38
John Kronus – 38
 Davey Boy Smith - 39
Johnny Grunge - 39
Vivian Vachon - 40
Jeep Swenson - 40
Brady Boone - 40
Terry Gordy - 40
Bertha Faye – 40
Billy Joe Travis – 40
Chris Benoit - 40
Larry Cameron - 41
Rick Rude - 41
Randy Anderson - 41
Bruiser Brody - 42
Miss Elizabeth - 42
Big Boss Man - 42
Earthquake – 42
Mike Awesome - 42
Biff Wellington – 42
Brian Adams (Crush) – 43
Ray Candy - 43
Nancy Benoit- 43
Dino Bravo – 44
Curt Hennig – 44
Bam Bam Bigelow - 45
Jerry Blackwell - 45
Junkyard Dog – 45
Hercules – 45
Andre the Giant – 46
Big John Studd - 46
Chris Adams - 46
Mike Davis – 46
Hawk - 46
Dick Murdoch- 49
Jumbo Tsuruta –49
Rocco Rock - 49
Sherri Martel - 49
Moondog Spot– 51
Ken Timbs– 53
Uncle Elmer– 54

Pez Whatley– 54
Eddie Graham- 55
Tarzan Tyler – 55
Haystacks Calhoun- 55
Giant Haystacks – 55
The Spoiler - 56
Kurt Von Hess - 56
Moondog King – 56
Gene Anderson – 58
Dr. Jerry Graham – 58
Bulldog Brown – 58
Tony Parisi - 58
Rufus R. Jones – 60
Ray Stevens – 60
Stan Stasiak – 60
Terry Garvin – 60
Boris Malenko - 61
Little Beaver – 61
Sapphire – 61
Shohei Baba – 61
Dick the Bruiser – 62
Wilbur Snyder - 62
George Cannon – 62
Karl Krupp – 62
Dale Lewis – 62
Gorilla Monsoon – 62
Hiro Matsuda - 62
Bad News Brown – 63
Bulldog Brower – 63
Wahoo McDaniel - 63

Wow! That's a lot of people who have passed on into eternity. WWE certainly has had its share of tragedy, and because of it has received a lot of attention and scrutiny in the media in recent years. I don't know if Miss Elizabeth in the list above, who died at age 42, is the same one who used to hang around wrestler Randy Savage. That lady was Elizabeth Heulette who has also passed. She was often referred to as "The Lovely Elizabeth." My brothers and I thought she was a total babe. She was really hot, and as kids we couldn't understand how a woman that beautiful could stand to be around a loser like the "Macho Man." Of course, now that I'm grown I fully understand. I know that all of the "fights" or "matches" were, and still are, completely scripted. After the wrestlers pretend to trash each other in the ring, they hang out together backstage having drinks and high-five-ing each other for good performances.

More recently, the WWE experienced, and is still dealing with, the loss of its star Chris Benoit. In a fit of depression and rage, the wrestler allegedly murdered both his wife Nancy, and his 7-year old son Daniel. High levels of testosterone were reported to have been found in the entertainer's bloodstream. In a CNN report I watched featuring neurosurgeon Dr. Sanjay Gupta, it was explained that high levels of unusual proteins were found in the deceased Chris' brain. Dr. Gupta and others on the program shared that brain damage from repeated head injuries, or steroid usage, might have contributed to Benoit's ultimately fatal behavior. After the said tragedies occurred, the WWE has become more strict on preventing employees from using steroids and other performance-enhancing substances, and has even instituted a wellness program which helps monitor the overall health of its wrestlers.

The subjects of war and peace have been expressed heavily in music and continue to be popular in songs today. I especially remember this to be true in the music I grew up listening to, particularly in the "heavy metal" genre. I am reminded of the songs "Peace Sells" by *Megadeth*, and *Slayer's* classic "War Ensemble." In the first, Dave Mustaine sarcastically asked the chorus question "Peace sells, but who's buying?" The video for that song featured clips of footage from various military conflicts America has been involved in.

In the latter, Tom Araya screams the chorus "Sport the war, war support. The sport is war, total war. When victory's a massacre. The final swing is not a drill. It's how many people I can kill." *Slayer* used the song "War Ensemble" as a dedication on their "Live, Decade of Aggression" album calling out support for all of "our troops in the Persian Gulf." Araya and company also touch on the subjects of war and death in the song "Mandatory Suicide." Which reminds me of the often-covered *Black Sabbath* classic "War Pigs" in which Ozzy wailed the dark poetry:

"Generals gathered in their forces. Just like witches at black masses. No more war pigs have the power. Hand of God has struck the hour. Oh Lord yeah!"

At the time of this writing, I am reminded further of contemporary movies and music that seem to capitalize on, or exploit, the sufferings and tragedies of others in order to "grease the palms" of those who made it. First, I recall award-winning director Oliver Stone's film *World Trade Center* (2006). Lest we forget the horror of one of America's saddest days,

Stone and the highly accomplished actor Nicholas Cage dramatically and effectively recreated the events of September 11, 2001. Before people scream at me for my criticism, I will say that I have seen the film and that the acting, special effects, and the production were excellent.

However, I know that the movie was not solely made as a big fund-raising project for the victims of 911. Yes, indeed, it has been reported that ten percent of opening weekend box office earnings went to related charities. That weekend, the cinematic feature earned over $70 million dollars. Five percent, or $3.5 million, was reportedly given to the building of a memorial at the "ground zero" site. The other half was reported to have been given to charities helping victims of 911. So, I'm saying that $3.5 million dollars is not anything to take lightly, but I can't help but be reminded that the makers of the movie kept the other $63 million for that weekend, plus all of the other earnings from ticket sales and DVD sales thereafter.

Who could forget controversial author and film-maker Michael Moore and his ambition to share with the world his disapproval of President George W. Bush and of the Republican Party? Of course his *Fahrenheit 911* was itself not a tragedy, but is simply his right as an American. However, was his movie really necessary? It could be viewed by some as a tasteless tactic of the author to assert his own political views. If that were the case, this writer believes that Moore's documentary trivializes the infamous attacks of 911 and is insensitive to the victims and the families who suffered loss from that tragedy.

Despite having only been screened in 868 theaters, Moore's movie earned about $24 million its opening weekend in the U.S. and Canada. It earned more than any other American documentary film on an opening weekend. The weekend of July 24, 2004, the movie surpassed the $100 million mark in box-office receipts. The film was released on DVDs and on VHS October 5, 2004, and it broke records for being the highest-selling documentary ever. About two million copies were sold on the first day. At the time of this writing, I could not find any evidence of Moore having given any earnings from his film to 911 victims. If that is the case, it's tragic.

He affectively asserted his disdain for "Dubya" and held him responsible for the terrorist attacks of September 11, 2001 in his widely viewed documentary. With mixed reviews and criticisms from both conservative as well as liberal minds, Moore seized the opportunity after the infamous attacks of 911 to expose what he claimed was the truth. Since the making of this movie, it has been closely monitored and scrutinized by politicians and film critics in an attempt to find more than just "relative truth."

I agree that everyone needs to know the truth about the persons and events responsible for creating the 911 tragedy, but I don't like to constantly be reminded of the pain and horror people suffered as a result. I am not saying whether I agree or not with Michael Moore and his cinematic story regarding the tragedy of September 11, 2001. I would need to obtain more information from other sources regarding this subject in order to develop a more rational opinion. However, I give Moore credit for producing a very thought-provoking film to entertain those who will listen. With that said, I wonder what will be the next tragedy exploited for people's entertainment.

CHAPTER SEVEN

Numbers

Numbers play a very integral role in the production of modern entertainment. Entertainment professionals in Los Angeles California know this all too well. In 1995 a group of civic leaders formed the LA Sports & Entertainment Commission (LASEC). The organization's website reported the following:

The 2005 Rose Bowl Game and the Tournament of Roses Parade generated over $200 million of direct spending and another $200 million of indirect spending to Los Angeles. Additionally, the 2005 City of Los Angeles Marathon generated $62 million of spending and continues to grow in size and prestige. The enormous revenues generated would not have been possible without the combined effort and support of corporate sponsors including: *American Express, Enterprise Rent-A-Car, Delta Airlines, Toyota, Sprint, and Spirit Aviation.*

Professional sports have a major economic impact on the city Los Angeles. Today's (2007 statistics from this author's search) pro sports industry generates an estimated $213 billion annually. This is twice the size of the automobile industry and bigger than all the public utilities put together. The movie business amasses over $31 billion nationwide and employs about 257,200 just in Los Angeles County. Sports travel is responsible for about $45 billion or 21% of the total sports industry's worth. This amount is defined as travel taken exclusively to attend or participate in a sporting event. Sport-related travel has increased 57% over the last five years, classifying two-fifths of U.S. adults as sports travelers. The average economic impact on a city hosting a major sporting event is more than $32 million. In recent years, these events have had the following economic impact on their host cities:

- NFL Superbowl $300 - 400 million and 100,000 visitors to the city
- PGA Ryder Cup $150 million
- MLB All-Star Game $60 million and 110,000 visitors
- NCAA Men's Basketball Final Four $50 million
- Gravity Games $23 million and 200,500 fans
- NCAA Women's Basketball Final Four $20.8 million
- NHL All-Star Game $10 million and over 100,00 visitors

Some of the sporting and entertainment events that have positively impacted the City of Los Angeles in recent years include:

Academy Awards, annual--$60.5 million (2000 event)

Avengers Arena Football--105,756 fans - 13,220 per game (2003)
Body Worlds 1 (July 2 - Jan 23, 2005)--665,190 attendance
Body Worlds 2 (Jan 29 - Mar 27, 2005)--264,916 attendance
Breeder's Cup Thoroughbred Championship (1993,1997, 2003)--$50 million (1993) and $60 million (1997)

City of Los Angeles Triathlon, annual since 2000--$8 million per event

Clippers Basketball--$24.6 million ticket revenue (1999-2000)
Dodgers Baseball--$41.2 million ticket revenue (1999-2000)
FIFA Women's World Cup Finals, 1999 and 2003--$30 million (1999)

Galaxy Soccer--330,000 fans- 21,983 per game (2003)
Grammy Awards--$26 million
Kings Hockey--$33.3 million ticket revenue (1999-2000)
Lakers Basketball--$63.1 million ticket revenue (1999-2000)
Latin Grammy Awards, 2000 and 2002--$16-$18 million per event; TV audiences of 7.5 million (2000), 4 million (2002)

Los Angeles Marathon, annual since 1986--$17+ million (2002 event); largest participatory event in the United States
Major League Soccer MLS Cup, 1998 and 2003--$5 million
Mercedes Benz Tennis Cup, annual--82,000 fans (2003 event)
NHL All-Star Game Weekend, 2002--$10+ million, 35,000 spectators per day
Nissan Open - PGA, annual--$29.6 million (2003 event)

Rose Parade and Rose Bowl,--$189 million direct; $181 million indirect (2005 event)
Summer Olympic Games, 1984--$3.29 billion
Super Bowl XXVII, 1993--$182 million
U.S. Figure Skating Championships (2002)--$25 million

It's funny... I've been to California to visit my best friends Aaron and Greg, who lived in Lake Tahoe. I've been all over California. Everywhere

I went and every day I've spent there, was an event. There was always a party or two to be found. There are professional musicians, actors and actresses, professional sports teams, an abundance of TV and radio stations, and exclusive resorts. There are great beaches, and renown slopes for snow skiing, there's Hollywood and Beverly Hills, casinos in Tahoe, many "adult entertainment," venues, incredible shopping malls, mountain trails for hiking and biking, several places to skateboard or surf, and world-famous cuisine at many restaurants. Please, don't mistake my comments as an advertisement for California. As a result of my many extensive travels, it has been my observation that California happens to be one of four largely populated states that supports entertainment. The others include New York, Texas, and Florida.

It has also been observed by this author that the most popular form of entertainment now, and perhaps ever in recorded history, is sex. Indeed, sex sells. Its evidence can be found almost everywhere. Its mediums include: television, music, Internet, magazines, books, sculptures, paintings, advertisements, DVDs and clothing. I observed while watching the History Channel, that the ancient Italian city of Pompeii had brothels and places which promoted sexual entertainment. Well-preserved, underneath the volcanic lava and ash which buried the city in the year 79 A.D, is such an establishment which contained explicit drawings and paintings on its walls and ceilings depicting sexual behaviors.

Evidence of similar forms of entertainment can be found in Christianity's Holy Bible. The writer Matthew accounts the circumstances which led to the death of the famous prophet John the Baptist. Chapter 3 recalls that Salome danced very sensually and provocatively for King Herod Antipas, and that having gazed upon her, he was enticed by her beauty. After Salome's sexy little dance, the king told her that she could have whatever she desired. After prompting from her mother Herodias, she asked for the head of John the Baptist on a platter.

Wow! All she did was entertain the Caesar with a dance! That little bit of pleasure ended in the tragic death of an innocent man. Okay, in the sake of fairness, the above would be true if you were inclined to believe that the Holy Bible is accurate as a historical document. At any rate, sex was as common a form of entertainment in the days of Christ, as it is now, if not more so, given the world's lack of technology (TV, Internet , and Radio) during the time when Christ lived on Earth.

A faith-based organization called Blazing Grace (BG) posted on its website in 2007 many statistics about pornography in America, and its consumption. However, the sources it sites for its statistical data are more secular in their natures. BG reported that according to *Internet Filter Review,* at $13.3 billion dollars, the 2006 revenues of the sex and pornography industries in the U.S were "bigger than the NFL, NBA, and Major League Baseball combined." Worldwide sex industry sales for 2006 were reported to have been $97 billion dollars. In comparison, Microsoft, who sells the operating systems used on most of the world's computers, only reported sales of $44.8 billion in 2006.

A 2000 *MSNBC* survey reported that "60% of all website visits are sexual in nature." As reported by BG, the approximate number of unique visitors to adult websites in 2006, per month, worldwide was 72 million. The number of American adults who regularly visit porn sites is 40 million (BG). An *LA Times Magazine*

article of 2002 reported that Hollywood released 11,000 "adult movies" that year –more than 20 times the mainstream movie production. The *National Opinion Research Letter* reported that one in four American adults surveyed in 2002 admitted to having seen an x-rated movie in the last year.

A 2005 *Focus on the Family* report revealed that the average teenager spent three to four hours per day watching television, or between 90 to 120 hours a month. It reported that 83% of the programming most frequently watched by adolescents contained some sexual content. In November of 2003, *CBS* reported that over 12,000 people in California were employed in the porn industry. They reported that in California alone, the porn industry "pays over $36 million in taxes every year." This writer would like to know if a study has ever been done to determine the amounts other individual American states collect in tax revenues from the porn industry each year. *The Barna Research* Group reported that 38 percent of adults surveyed believed it was 'morally acceptable' to look at pictures of nudity or explicit sexual behavior.

CBS News reported that in 2002 *Comcast,* the nation's largest cable television company, earned $50 million from "adult programming." All of America's top cable operators, from *Cablevision* to *Time Warner,* distributed sexually explicit materials to their subscribers. *DirecTV* ,which is owned by *Hughes Technology,* a subsidiary of *General Motors,* has earned considerable revenues from its sale of adult products. According to Dennis McAlpine of *McAlpine Associates,* the satellite television provider *DirecTV* annually earns "probably a couple hundred million, maybe as much as $500 million, off of adult entertainment, in a broad sense."

Lastly, The American Academy of Pediatrics' journal *Pediatrics* reported in Volume 107, Number 2, of February 2001 that "content analyses show that children and teenagers continue to be bombarded with sexual imagery and innuendos in programming and advertising."

The United States Department of Labor's own Bureau of Labor Statistics reported some alarming numbers when I visited its Internet site on July 3, 2007. That day the agency reported statistics on consumer spending patterns for both the U.S. as a whole as well as some statistics for individual metropolitan areas. The site reported statistics for the year 2004 to 2005. That year, the average American spent 5.8 percent of his or her income on healthcare, 5.1 percent on entertainment, and just a measly 2.1 percent on education! It was reported that the average American spent more than twice as much of his or her income on entertainment, as was spent on education! The bureau also reported that the average American spent almost as much on entertainment that year as that person did for healthcare!

I learned some interesting perspectives about the music industry from radio DJ Anthony Proffitt who is, perhaps, better known to listeners as "Roach." At the time of our interview, he was managing a rock radio station in Jacksonville, Florida. However, when we first met in the 1990s he was a DJ for the popular *94.3 FM Extreme Radio* in Knoxville, Tennessee. Anyhow, Roach explained to me how the Internet and technology has drastically affected numbers in the radio industry. Hold told me that a radio station that might have had a staff of 100 twenty years ago would likely have a staff of around five currently. He said "Most radio stations today are at least 80 percent smaller in staff numbers than they were 20 years ago due to computer technology, automated equipment, and the Internet. Corporate downsizing in today's not-so-robust economy has also been a factor. From a business perspective, companies who own radio stations don't usually want to put 20 people on the payroll as Djs when they can buy one automated, computer-driven system that can do all of the work of those 20 persons instead. Radio stations aren't what they were when we were kids (Roach and I)."

Roach also shared about how certain companies had been buying up radio stations across the U.S. and dominating what America heard on the airwaves. Which reminds me of a conversation I had with music guru Gary Mitchell. Gary has owned several music clubs in my hometown of Knoxville through the years. He has also owned clubs in other states as well. One night I had the pleasure of speaking with Gary for about an hour and a half at a bar he owned called *Tonic*. It was quite unusual as Gary was usually pretty busy and was not noted for being talkative. But then again, he was talking with ME! *smirk*

Gary currently owns *The Valarium* in Knoxville. It is commonly host to hard rock bands and popular music. Anyhow, Gary shared with me a lot of personal perspectives about the music and entertainment business and mentioned how some corporations had not only purchased radio stations around America, but had also bought many of the clubs and establishments around the country that he has often had to compete with. So, indeed numbers and market shares are important factors to consider when working in the entertainment industry.

Like my graduate statistics professor Dr. Skuylar Huck at the University of Tennessee, I would also be interested to know how large the sample size was in the Department of Labor's study, and also where the participants in the study were found. Were there more participants in some areas than in others? Were participants more wealthy or more economically challenged? Nevertheless, the website reported numbers for the United States as a whole, but it also included reports on the year 2004 to 2005 expenditures for Baltimore, St. Louis, San Diego, Denver, and Pittsburg.

Interestingly, it was reported in this study that although the average income, before taxes, in San Diego was almost $4,000 more per year than in Denver, citizens in Denver spent, on average, $574 more per year on entertainment than in San Diego. However, it is reported on the site that "Baltimore area households allocated a significantly smaller portion of their budgets to entertainment (4.3 percent) when compared to the average household in the U.S. (5.1 percent). Likewise, a typical household in San Diego allocated a significantly below-average share to entertainment (4.4 percent).

I read an interesting article online, in August of 2007, by the writer Sean Deveney for the magazine SportingNews. It was about the top ten NBA players of "limited ability but bounteous salary." I found it interesting, because there were numerous examples of where consumers have been ripped off by the costs they paid to be entertained. Since it is my personal bias as a writer not to write anything negative about persons, I decided to change the names of the players mentioned in Mr. Deveney's article and to let readers have the fun of figuring out which players I am writing about. Also, it is my opinion that professional athletes are mostly paid too much. I think high ticket prices just to go and watch folks "live" is lame.

The first player discussed in that article was Miner Diggs of the Denver Nuggets. Diggs was reported to have been paid $13 million after having only played two games for Denver. It was reported that he signed an $86 million deal, in spite of recovering from knee surgery at the time when the Nuggets signed him. Was the high-altitude air in Denver thin that day or what? Spankey Yankee of the New York Nicks is reported to have had his "lowest numbers since his rookie season," with his 41.5 percent shooting. He is 30 years old and is reportedly earning more than $17 million a year.

Next on the list is Bloaduh Sax of the Utah Jazz. He is reported to have gotten "teary-eyed," and cried, in the first round of last year's playoffs, in spite of his having been paid $13.7 million. It was reported that Mookie Stroller of the Miami Heat has had his share of rough times recently. He was robbed at gunpoint in his Chicago home. However, it would be wrong to ignore his poor performance. "He shot 39.7 percent from the field, which put him 355th in the league. He was 43.8 percent from the free-throw line, which was 432nd. He shot 27.5 percent from the 3-point line, or 232nd." Some would argue that Stroller has been very unproductive, given the fact that he has a contract for $8.5 million.

Another arguably low-producing, and overpaid NBA player is Ripe Lemons of the Portland Trailblazers. In the 2003-2004 season, he played in just 17 games for the Boston Celtics. Lemons reportedly wrote a letter to Celtics fans apologizing for his poor level of productivity. However, he did not offer to give back any of the millions he made. He was in Portland averaging a meager 3.7 points per games, but still got paid just under $12 million. For $12 million, I might be motivated to try just a little harder, if I were Lemons. The six-feet and seven-inches tall Mark Thorn of the New York Knicks is a forward who shot only 39.8 percent. He was perfectly healthy, but averaged just 3 points and 2.7 rebounds in 12.5 minutes.

Since I'm on the subject of sports, let's not just pick on the NBA. Let's examine the NFL. I didn't change any names, but I found the following information and numbers to be quite interesting:

On September 5, 2007 The New York Giants and New York Jets officially broke ground on a new $1.3 billion stadium. The 82,500-seat complex is being privately financed by the Giants and the Jets. It marks the first time in NFL history that a single stadium will permanently house two different franchises.

"This partnership between the Jets and Giants is unique not only for the NFL but in all of sports," NFL Commissioner Roger Goodell said. "Ensuring that the stadium would feel like home to both teams and both groups of fans was our goal and also one of the biggest challenges in the design of the stadium," Giants Executive Vice President Steve Tisch said. " Placed adjacent to the existing Giants Stadium, the new facility is scheduled to be completed prior to the 2010 season and will host 20 games each year.

The unnamed stadium will include a 400-foot long, 40-foot high panel called "the Great Wall," upon which either team's logo will be featured.

"Our ability to transform the building overnight also extends to meet the needs not only of each team on game day, but can become a neutral building on non-game days," Tisch said.

The architectural designs for a 2.1 million-square-foot facility were unveiled. The complex, which occupies 40 acres, also includes a 300,000-square-foot outdoor plaza for tailgating and a new rail facility which will connect the stadium to New York's Penn Station beginning in February 2009.

How could one possibly forget the entertaining sport of golf? While it may not be much to watch on TV, or maybe even in person, it is still capable of generating large sums of money. Such has been the case for Tiger Woods, who arguably is the best golfer in history. Dan Wetzel of Yahoo reported on September 4, 2007 that Tiger Woods "has the world's greatest employer-funded retirement pack." I found the following after reading his article:

If Woods keeps winning at his current rate, enjoys a nine percent annual return and captures just seven FedEx Cups in his career, he could reach $1 billion in retirement payouts courtesy of the PGA Tour. If the PGA right this moment started handing Tiger a dollar bill every second of every minute of every day, it wouldn't reach a billion until 2039. If Tiger Woods were to win 11 FedEx Cups, it means he would have an estimated approximate retirement worth of:

2007: $123.1 million
2008: $112.9 million
2010: $95 million
2011: $87.2 million
2013: $73.1 million
2015: $61.5 million
2017: $51.8 million

That totals up to $604.6 million when he is 60.

At this point, according to PGA Tour spokesman Bob Cook, Woods would have to start making withdrawals that would empty the account in five years. The payments are made monthly based on a yearly recalculated number. The decreasing money, however, will continue to accrue interest during the 60 months and will earn an estimated additional $114.7 million, according to Morgan Stanley's Yellen.

That gives Woods $718.7 million in FedEx Cup money alone. Add on the $300 million in payouts from the other, original pension plans and you have $1,018,700,000. And this is a number Woods can easily shatter in any number of ways – more victories, longer career, better investment performance. So there's his $1 billion.

Lastly, but certainly not least is the digital entertainment industry. I mean every form of art and entertainment is available in a digital medium. We are living in the age of video games and computerized multimedia. Just look around and you can find in the electronics section at department stores, such as Target or Walmart, demos and advertisements for games such as *Guitar Hero* or *Rock Star*. To give readers some clue as to how popular video games can be, and the enormous amounts of profit that can be made from video game sales, I have compiled a list of some best-selling video games of all time. My information was found mostly on the Internet from the writer Ben Silverman. Some best-selling game franchises in 2007 were:

7. **Gran Turismo**
Units Sold: 47 Million
Defining Game: Gran Turismo (PSOne)

6. **Donkey Kong**
Units Sold: 48 Million

5. **Grand Theft Auto**
Units sold: 65 million

4. **Final Fantasy**
Units sold: 75 million

3. **The Sims**
Units sold: 90 million

2. **Pokemon**
Units sold: 164 million

1. **Mario**
Units sold: 195 million
Defining game: Super Mario Brothers

Spanning an illustrious 25-year career, the world's most famous plumber has also become its most successful. Starting with the 1983 arcade classic Mario Brothers, a Mario game has graced every Nintendo console system ever released, from the classic NES to the more contemporary Virtual Boy. Like a Renaissance man, he's had more successful releases than The Beatles. His life has spawned entire genres (Mario Kart and Super Mario 64) and reinvented old ones (Super Paper Mario). Along the way, the famous Italian character has grossed Nintendo in upwards of $8 billion. Readers may recall another famous plumber who received much media attention during the battle for the Presidency between Barack Obama and John McCain. The plumber in question is "Joe the Plumber." Perhaps, Mr. Joe needs to market his own Joe the Plumber video game. After all, Mario was named after real-life Nintendo of America office landlord Mario Segale. What's it going to hurt to have another video game about an average Joe?

CHAPTER EIGHT

Rock the Vote

Entertainment and politics…Or is it, the politics of entertainment? Many political persons support entertainment, and vice versa. Evidence of the marriage between politics and entertainment can be easily found on a daily basis. Just look at the number of governmental leaders in America who have directly been involved in entertainment. Take, for example, California Governor Arnold Schwarzenegger. He has acted professionally in several highly acclaimed movies including *Conan the Barbarian, The Terminator, Commando, Predator, Kindergarten Cop,* and *Total Recall.* Another previous California Governor, Ronald Reagan, acted in numerous less-acclaimed movies, but went on to become the President of the United States. Reagan is credited mostly for his helping to end the "cold war" between the U.S. and Russia, and for spearheading the deconstruction of the Berlin Wall, which led to the reunion of East and West Germany.

Former presidential candidate, and New Jersey Senator, Bill Bradley played basketball prior to his political career, and he helped lead the New York Knicks to two NBA titles. Former Minnesota Governor Jesse Ventura wrestled in what became the WWE, and after he left wrestling, he acted in movies including *Predator, Demolition Man, Batman & Robin, No Holds Barred,* and *The Running Man,* prior to his entering politics. Men are not exclusively the only entertainers who have actively been involved in politics. Through the years singer and actress Barbara Streisand (*Meet the Fockers*) has campaigned for, and generally supported the Democratic Party. She even campaigned for, and supported, former Massachusetts Governor Michael Dukakis in his run for President in 1988.

Singer Bette Midler has campaigned for and widely publicized her support for the Democratic Party. Stevie Nicks and her band Fleetwood Mac performed at the Democratic National Convention in 1992. Singer Natalie Merchant had the song "These Are Days" by her band *10,000 Maniacs* played at the 43rd Democratic National Convention. But wait, just when readers thought that only the Democrats get musicians to support them, think again. I personally recall listening to the old R&B group *The Drifters* perform at the "Duncan Family BBQ" in 2002.

Republican Congressman John Duncan, Jr., or "Jimmy," and his family held their annual BBQ at the Civic Coliseum in Knoxville. At that time, I worked with his sister Becky who invited me, because my grandparents (Hester) were neighbors with her parents, and her brother, and her father John Duncan, Sr. was also a congressman. Anyhow, they entertained thousands of guests at the Knoxville Civic Coliseum with good BBQ and music by African-American crooners *The Drifters*. The Drifters were the group responsible for the 1964 hit song "Under the Boardwalk." Among the guests that evening, whom I met and spoke briefly with were former Presidential Candidate Lamar Alexander, at that time Governor Don Sundquist, and former House Majority leader Senator Bill Frist.

Obviously, this is just one example of how some Republicans liked to entertain folks. Congressman Duncan's father was also a congressman, and my grandmother (Mary) campaigned for him. She and my grandfather (Bill) considered John to be a good friend. Even though my grandparents were staunch Republicans (Grandmother campaigned for Nixon), they still had a few friends who were Democrats, and had some they generally respected. For example, my grandfather was good friends with former Democratic Presidential Candidate Senator Estes Kefauver. Senator Kefauver invited he and my father (Jr.) to Washington, DC and entertained them with a grand tour, which included introducing them to then Vice-President Richard Nixon. Now, why can't folks be less partisan and get along like they did in those days? Anyhow, I'd be pretty darn entertained if a US senator invited me to DC and gave me a tour of the White House, the Capitol, and the House of Representatives! Plus, my grandpa and my dad both got a VIP ride on the United States Capitol Subway System with the Senator.

Okay, so are you wondering what all of the rambling about my grandparents' political connections is really about? I thought this short spill would be a little ENTERTAINING for some readers! A better example of how politics and entertainment are connected, perhaps, would be in the personal recollections shared with me and others at a dinner in which Tony Coelho was the featured speaker. The dinner was held as a fund-raiser for the Epilepsy Foundation of East Tennessee in Knoxville. At that time (2003), Tony was the President of the Epilepsy Foundation of America. During his speech, the charismatic speaker shared with his audience how he, a liberal Democrat, was actually introduced to politics by his conservative Republican friend, the legendary comedian Bob Hope.

Mr. Coelho told of how a Catholic leader introduced him to Bob, after he was denied being allowed to become a priest. Tony shared how he had worked for some years for Mr. Hope in California, and that Bob helped support him in his run for Congress. Mr. Coelho was elected in 1978 as a Congressman representing California. He left Congress in 1989, but he became the primary author of the Americans with Disabilities Act (ADA) in 1990. In 1994, he was appointed by President Clinton to serve as the Chairman of the President's Committee on Employment of Persons with Disabilities. In 1999, Coelho returned to politics when Vice President Al Gore asked him to serve as the General Chairman of his presidential campaign.

A more direct connection, perhaps, between entertainment and politics can be found between Al Gore and his connection with the music industry. In the 1990s, Gore's wife Tipper founded the Parents Music Resource Center, or PMRC, which encouraged the packaging of some music with parental advisory labels to aid parents in monitoring the content of the music their children want to listen to. More recently, is Gore's popularity for his award-winning movie documentary *An Inconvenient Truth*, which discusses the state of Earth's current environment. Vice President Gore briefly presented his movie, and his views on the Earth's environment, to a captive audience at The 2007 MTV Video Music Awards.

Following that, he and Kevin Wall organized a series of worldwide concerts that all took place in various countries on "7-7-07" to promote awareness about global warming and environmental issues. Live Earth Concerts on MSN.com "were the most watched entertainment event in online history." MSN delivered 30 million streams and more than 8 million people worldwide experienced live online coverage. Other entertaining politics, during the production of this book, has been the live coverage of the Democratic and Republican presidential debates. Traditional television news programs have covered the debates between the candidates, but with the utilization of the Internet during current election cycles, people around the globe have a unique voice and participation in the political process by being able to broadcast their questions for candidates, along with personal comments, on websites such as YouTube and MySpace.

For myself and others who like to watch politicians debate current issues, it was a real treat to watch Obama and McCain hash things out in their last two "town hall-style" debates before Obama was elected to be President. It was a dream come true for many comedians and satirists. The NBC Network pounced on the opportunity to share political comedy by airing a special episode of its program *Saturday Night Live* on a

Thursday evening following the debate between the two candidates. In a classic crass and sarcastic style Saturday Night Live is known for, actors imitated both of the candidates and also the various citizens who questioned the candidates during the said debate. Following that special episode, clips of it surfaced all over the Internet. Interestingly, Vice Presidential Candidate Sarah Palin made an appearance on Saturday Night live following the last debate between McCain and Obama.

Another famous entertainer involved in the occupation of politics is U.S. Senator Fred Thompson. Like his Republican colleagues Governor Arnold Swartzenegger and President Ronald Reagan, Thompson has acted in numerous movies. In contrast, Thompson worked in politics first before professionally acting, unlike Reagan and Swartzenegger who both worked professionally as actors prior to their workings in politics. But what's the difference between politics and acting? *smirk* Seriously, I know I happened to mention three Republicans, which is a coincidence, but it could be argued that persons in politics, regardless of their party affiliations are ALL actors in some capacity at one time or another. With that said, let's examine some famous thespians who are Democrats and are involved in politics.

Actor Michael J. Fox has openly and publicly expressed his support for the Democratic party. This could be, perhaps, because more Democrats than Republicans have supported his work and his views on stem-cell research. In 2000 the actor renown for his work in the movie *Back to the Future,* and in the TV sitcom *Growing Pains,* was diagnosed with the debilitating Parkinson's Disease. After his diagnosis, the actor has aggressively sought the help of the American government to help fund research and treatments that could lead to cures of that disease.

It has been reported by various sources, including the Internet site, isteve.com that Oscar-winning actors, actresses, and directors have traditionally given most of their support to the Democratic Party. In 2003, they gave about forty times more money to Democrats than to Republicans. Thirty-one Oscar winners gave $381,000 to the Democratic Party in 2003, versus only seven who gave $9,000 to the Republican party. Big donors included actor Michael Douglas ($98,000), actor Tom Hanks ($27,000), and director/producer Stephen Speilberg ($165,000). In 2000, Haim Saban of Saban Entertainment (*Mighty Morphin Power Rangers*) gave $1.3 million to Democrats.

Lastly, I am reminded of the entertaining and entrepreneurial talk-show diva Oprah Winfrey and her support for Barack Obama during his 2008 run for President. It has been widely televised that Winfrey personally organized a dinner to benefit the campaign for Obama.

Tickets to the event sold for a minimum of $2,300 apiece. The event reportedly earned more than $3,000,000 for Barack Obama's bid to become President.

This amount is nothing to "sneeze at." However, it was very affordable for Oprah Winfrey to support Obama, as she is reported to have been worth over $1.5 billion at the time when she held this fund raiser. Perhaps, Ms. Winfrey could continue in her spirit of generosity and use her own Book-of-the-Month Club to showcase support for a poor, but deserving, writer named James Hester. *grin* Wow! Now wouldn't that be something? If Oprah would invest some of her time and resources to help showcase the talents of a bright young man who worked hard and overcame his adversity, I'm should she would reap a great harvest.

She would gain many viewers, receive great ratings, and get a sure profit return on her investment. Oh, and let us not forget that if she chose to support Mr. Hester's campaign to become the President of The Coolness Foundation, she would be admired by millions for supporting his passionate, selfless altruism, and becoming his good buddy. The world would applaud and adore her for supporting one of humanity's greatest contributors. World hunger would end, or we could at least have a really big BBQ! Every disease and sickness known would be cured! Or at least the pharmaceutical companies would give every man, woman, and child on Earth free samples of Wellbutrin, so we could all die happy while they gain from the charitable tax write-offs! Politicians and lawyers would all agree to attend courses on "learning how to be honest," or as a rule of law be required to serve time as inmates in state prisons! James Hester for President! James! James! James!

CHAPTER NINE

Divine Media

One cannot deny that religions, faiths, or spiritual philosophies have all influenced the lives of entertainers and their works. The subjects of faith, spirituality, and religion, are available in various mediums that can often be considered entertaining. Take for example Islam, and the millions of persons who call themselves Muslims and subscribe to that faith. There are some famous entertainers who claim, or have claimed, to be Muslims. First, I am reminded of a popular musician whom I wanted to meet once when he played at the music club Moose's Music Hall in Knoxville, Tennessee.

The singer and songwriter known as Everlast performed at Moose's once while I was in college. Ultimately, I was not able to attend that show, but I learned from the club's manager James O'Neill that Everlast was a devout Muslim at that time. James told me that he wouldn't have been able to get "anybody backstage that night," because the artist requested no one be allowed into his dressing room before and after the show. James said that before the show, Everlast spent a "considerable amount of time" backstage on his knees and face bowing toward Mecca while praying. O'Neill said he offered to get drinks for the entertainer, and Everlast requested only bottled water, but adamantly forbid there being any alcohol in his personal area. O'Neill shared that he was "impressed by him." He said "We (the club) always have to be courteous and respectful of any of our artists or guests here, and we try to accommodate their wishes."

Another example of faith and religion in entertainment is the movie *The Passion of the Christ*. The Internet encyclopedia called *WIKIPEDIA* reported that the film's production budget was $25 million and its printing and advertising budget was $10 million. In the U.S, the motion picture's gross earnings were nearly $380 million, while worldwide they were about $610 million. Those numbers are indeed noteworthy for a film inspired by actor and director Mel Gibson's Christian faith. Other forms of media considered by this writer to be entertainment include Christian TV networks TBN and Daystar.

From an objective perspective on faith-based entertainment, one cannot deny the popularity and numbers generated by the Lakewood

Church on TBN. The Houston-based church led by pastor, best-selling author, and televangelist Joel Osteen is the first church in America to average more than 30,000 worshipers in its attendance weekly. It is also estimated that over seven million faithful watch Osteen's message weekly on TBN. The network also features local, and grassroots, programs at various stations around the world.

The network's Internet site reports "TBN is the world's largest religious network and America's most watched faith network. Each day TBN offers 24 hours of commercial-free inspirational programming that appeals to people in a wide variety of denominations. Beginning in 1973 as a single UHF station in southern California, TBN now reaches every major continent via 54 satellites and more than 12,500 television and cable affiliates worldwide. In the United States, TBN is available to 92 percent of the total households. Its website receives more than 27 million visitors monthly."

As mentioned previously in this book, I once graced the airwaves of TBN with my funky trumpet blasts of praise. Okay, I don't think I really sounded good or looked good, but it wasn't about me or anyone else. I was on the show to help members and visitors at Community Fellowship Church (CFC) in Dalton, Georgia to praise the Lord Jesus Christ. The looks, the sounds, the sermon, and all the people were second to worshiping the Lord. Honestly, I was not well prepared for this event. Because I had only learned about it a week in advance and had not practiced the music much with the musicians, the Music Director asked me not to put a microphone on my horn. It was done just in case, so bad notes on my trumpet wouldn't saturate the airwaves.

Well, after the service, the Manager of the local TBN station came to me and told me I sounded great! Her name was Onya Richter. She said my playing was "anointed" and she invited me and the other musicians at CFC to stop by the studio sometime to record and mix some stuff. Wow! A short time later, the episode I briefly appeared on was played on TBN. I was indeed on the TBN Network for a local episode that was played on stations in households in North Georgia and in the Greater Chattanooga, Tennessee area.

Yes, I was on the same network which features the legendary Joel Osteen. However, prior to this book I have never been a guest for any program hosted by Osteen. Hint...Hint... The same commercials for all of the internationally acclaimed shows were aired before and after the program I was on, but the program itself was only for the local viewing area. TBN works like most secular, non-faith based networks do in that it has many local television stations and channels. Each station chooses which popular, widely syndicated programs to air, but also allots time for programs focused on its own specific viewing area.

This became very clear to me one day when I was tutoring students at a school in Ellijay, Georgia. The school was a good 45 minute drive east from my home. One afternoon I was tutoring some middle school students in math and a girl said to me: "Mr. Hester, I saw you on TV!" It's a funny memory, because I had to stop and think about it for a moment in order to remember. "What channel did you see me on?" I asked. She responded gleefully "My momma was watching a Black preacher on TBN. It was from some church in Dalton and you were on stage playing trumpet. You were gettin' down!"

All of the sudden I was a celebrity to a group of kids struggling to learn math. I was glad one saw me on that show and not some program with hidden cameras following me around and exposing my screw ups! I am far from perfect, but I am proud of my Christian faith. I might not be the "model Christian," (whatever that's supposed to mean) but I will not deny or try to hide my beliefs. I prefer to share my faith and beliefs rather than try to force Christ on anyone. If folks would read the Bible and study it, they might find that Christ never forced himself on anyone or spoke harshly against folks who did not believe him.

Other examples of faith and religion found in entertainment can be heard in popular songs. Take for example the artists *R.E.M.* The alternative rock band had a successful hit single with it's song "Losing My Religion." In spite of the depth and subject matter of the song, it has been reported that R.E.M's guitarist wrote it while he was watching TV and at the same time learning to play the mandolin. It contains the resonating words "That's me in the corner. That's me in the spotlight losing my religion." The song peaked in its popularity on the Billboard Top 100 Chart at number 4. It was released in February of 1991 on the *Out of Time* album. The album sold 4.2 million copies in the U.S. alone and went on to sell an additional 12 million worldwide by 1996. This reminds me of other songs by great rock bands.

I remember some controversy surrounded two of my favorite "grunge" bands from the 1990s. First, I recall the tune "Jesus Christ Pose" by Chris Cornell's old band *Soundgarden*. It was one of the hits on the band's platinum-selling album "Bad Motor Finger." I have a copy of the video for that song. The video featured incredible footage of Cornell and his bandmates in the middle of a desert with all sorts of surreal time-lapsed photography. In it, the singer holds his arms out open like he's being crucified while yelling "You stare at me in your Jesus Christ Pose! Arms are out wide, like it's the coming of the Lord! And you swear to

me that you don't want to be my friend, but you're staring at me like I... Like I need to be saved!"

The latter I recall seemed more direct to folks and had many Christians screaming. The song I'm referring to is "Man in the Box." It was written and recorded by *Alice in Chains* and is found on the album "Facelift." It was one of the songs I learned to play on the guitar, as did many other depressed, zit-faced, boys in those days. Of course it was a masterpiece of misery that bludgeoned the ears of listeners with guitarist Jerry Cantrell's "drop-D" fretwork. That combined with the wails of the late, great, Layne Stayley was a sure recipe to make any angst-filled adolescent give it a listen.

In the piece Stayley whined "Feed my eyes! (chanting) Can you sow them shut... Jesus Christ! (chanting) Deny your maker... He who tries will be wasted! Feed my eyes! (chanting) Now you've sewn them shut..." I'm not sure what Alice in Chains was saying, but to me it said that sometimes a person can be stuck seeing things a certain way to where someone has "feed that person's eyes" by showing him or her another perspective. One can take the words "now you've sewn them shut" to mean "now you've made me think this way permanently." Or those words can mean "now you've changed my mind about life and about Jesus Christ."

However, one chooses to interpret the song, it is indeed a powerful medium of expression by the said artists. I feel it important to note, however, that Jerry Cantrell some years later on his first solo CD "Boggy Depot" recorded a song about the grace of Jesus (might not have been Christ) called "Jesus Hands." I asked Mr. Cantrell about the song when we met and if it had to do with his own personal faith, but out of respect for his privacy I will not discuss his answers, as our discussion was unofficial and we were just casually hanging out.

It would be irresponsible of me not mention country legend Johnny Cash's expression of his Christian faith in the song "Spiritual." In it, Cash moans in his signature baritone voice the words "Jesus. I don't wanna die alone. My love wasn't true. Now all I have is you. Jesus. Precious Jesus. I don't wanna die alone." It was one of the songs featured on Cash's CD "Unchained." Interestingly, Flea from the band *Red Hot Chili Peppers* played bass on the recording of the tune. I don't know if his faith had a part in his deciding whether or not to perform on that song. Cash's song reminds me of other contemporary music legends who had or have Christian faiths.

Take for example former Korn guitarist Brian "Head" Welch and his decision to leave that group due to his personal Christian faith and convictions. The artist shared in an interview I watched on the TBN network about just how terrible being a celebrity can sometimes be. He told about his struggles as a single father raising a little girl, while at the same time self-destructing on heroin. He shared about the process of his coming to have faith and how his Christian faith had saved him from death and self-defeat. His faith inspired him to write the book "Save Me From Myself" and to write and record a heavy Christian rock album. Other secular entertainers who have had or currently have Christian faiths include: Elvis Presley, Dolly Parton, Carrie Underwood, Curt Warner, Carlos Santana, Bono, Chuck Norris, MC Hammer, B.B. King, Charlie Daniels, Lou Brock, Alice Cooper, James Brown, T Bone, P.O.D, Jane Fonda, Lenny Kravitz, Ray Charles, RED, Skillet, Amy Grant, Karl Denson, Switchfoot, Cuba Gooding, Jr. and many others.

Although I have a strong faith in Jesus Christ, I want to be fair and mention some other entertainers and their faiths as well. First, let us contemplate for a moment the growing number of popular artists and entertainers who describe themselves as members of the Church of Scientology. First, I am reminded of the accomplished actors John Travolta and Tom Cruise. Both have discussed in televised interviews their support of the Church of Scientology and its founder L. Ron Hubbard's views. Both have shared about how their faiths have affected their professional work, as well as their personal lives. Although her late father recorded gospel albums and professed having a Christian faith, Lisa Marie Presley and her husband Michael Lockwood are both reported to be members of the Church of Scientology.

Some Buddhists entertainers I can recall, whose works I have admired and respected include Kurdt Cobain. I once saw in a television report that my late grunge hero of the 1990s had a small shrine and a statue of Buddha in his house. Although they were born and raised Jewish, I am told that some of the members of the famous band the *Beastie Boys* are Buddhist. I think I read in Spin Magazine that Adam Yauch is a Buddhist. One of my favorite soul singers, Tina Turner, has been reported on Wikipedia's website to be Buddhist.

The late reggae great Bob Marley was a Rastafarian. I met some members of his former group *The Wailers* and some of them subscribed to the Rastafarian faith. A Rastafarian at a festival once told me that his faith is actually a sect of gnostic Christians. He explained that they have non-traditional beliefs about Christ that have not been canonized or accepted by most other Christian sects, but nonetheless they have faith in Christ. Others I have enjoyed listening to include the "Rasta-punk" band *Bad Brains*. The group expressed its faith in the mellow praise song "Yes Jah," but has also rocked hard in hits such as the song "Rise."

Returning to Islam, one may remember boxing great Muhammad Ali who could "float like a butterfly and sting like a bee" when he was in the ring. How could I forget watching a VH1 segment about the singer and songwriter known as *Cat Stevens*? His dedication to his faith prompted him to give up the spotlight and glamor of a successful secular music career in turn to serve Allah. He even changed his name to Yusef Islam. It has been reported that he wanted God to receive glory and not himself. Also reported was that hip-hop artist Busta Rhymes was a Muslim. Ironically, I saw such reported in an Internet article after controversy over one of his songs called "Arab Money." Professional NBA player Kareem Abdul Jabar is a legend I grew up watching as a kid. I admired his trademark shot the "sky hook." Let's not forget big Shaq either. Shaquille O'Neill is one of my favorite NBA players. It's not everyday that a man his size has so much agility and skill.

Again, I have to mention one of rap and hip-hop music's legends. His name is Carlton Ridenhour. Readers may recognize him better as Chuck D, the frontman for *Public Enemy*. It has been reported that he was a Muslim. In the hit "Bring the Noise," he called Nation of Islam President Louis Farrakhan "a prophet" whom people should listen to. However, many average, mainstream, Muslims consider Farrakhan and his sect to be radical and not a true form of Islam. Since I am not Muslim and this book does not focus on faith and religion, I will save my opinions about the Nation of Islam for another time and place in sh'Allah (God willing).

Not wanting to lump them all together, because there are some differences, there are some musicians who subscribe to Pagan, Witchcraft, Voodoo, or Wiccan beliefs. It is my understanding that hard rockers *Type O Negative* practice living by many ancient Celtic traditions that are Pagan in origin. I seem to recall hearing this in interviews with the band's members. Magazine and television interviews report that Sully Erna from the band *Godsmack* subscribes to and practices Wiccan and Voodoo philosophies.

Such inspired him to write and record the popular song "Voodoo." It has an otherworldly feel as Erna chants the words "I'm not the one who's so far away, as I feel the snakebite enter my veins. Never do I want to be here again, and I don't remember why I came." Lastly, Jasin Todd, formerly of Shinedown as mentioned earlier, told me he practiced having a Wiccan faith and lifestyle. This was represented by his signature pentagram belt buckle he wore the various times I met and spoke with him. Even though I don't subscribe to the same faith as Todd , I still respect his thoughts and views and it was a real pleasure speaking with him.

From my many studies about religion and faith, I have also learned that many famous entertainers have been members of the Church of Satan. Now hold on everyone! It's been obvious so far that I am a Christian, so let's not misconstrue my discussion on this particular philosophy as being one to condone or support it. However, in the sake of fairness and to give readers an accurate recollection of my experiences in the entertainment industry, I am going to speak briefly about this group as well. For starters, let us examine this church's founder Anton LaVey. Both before and after establishing his beliefs in the form of a church, LaVey worked heavily in the entertainment industry.

Anton LaVey began entertaining folks in traveling circuses as a keyboard player and a magician's assistant. It has also been reported that he worked in several carnivals and freakish "sideshows." LaVey also performed as an actor making cameo appearances in commercials and in movies. Because of that I used to believe that I saw him in the 1980 movie *Flash Gordon* when I was a boy. I, along with many others, mistakenly thought he played the role of Ming the Merciless in that movie. However, I have learned since then that the part was actually played by a very similar looking fellow named Max Von Sydow.

It was only years later that I came to recognize LaVey more easily, as he kept the same bald head and goatee mustache as his signature look. I remember when I was in high school seeing him in a commercial for MTV. Also during my high school years, I remember reading an interview with him that was published in *Rolling Stone* magazine. The reason I remember reading it is because my favorite band at the time, *Guns 'n Roses* ,was photographed together on the cover. GNR was the only reason why I picked up that magazine. Nevertheless, I found the article on LaVey interesting, and the photos of this famous bald man have not been forgotten.

LaVey is reported to have had many friends and followers in the entertainment industry. For starters, it has been rumored that he and the late actress / pinup girl *Marylin Monroe* dated for a time and were lovers. To this day, it is still a mystery as to who and what killed Marylin Monroe. It is believed by some that her tragic fate was the result of the diva having sold her soul to Satan in exchange for fame and fortune. Of course, I caution readers to study the history of this woman's life themselves in order to find what they believe to be the truth about her, as I am not an expert on the matter.

A more-recent member of the *Church of Satan*, as he proclaimed in various writings and interviews, is the shocker-rocker *Marylin Manson*. Various sources report that the "antichrist superstar" was good friends with Anton LaVey, who personally ordained Manson and made him a "reverend" in his church. However, when I was a professional counselor some years ago I had a Satanic priest I worked with share with me his faith and his knowledge about Marylin Manson. The said priest told me me that "Marylin Manson does not see himself as a spokesperson for Satanism or any particular faith."

By now readers might be asking themselves "What about the Jews James?" They are both an ethnic group as well as a religious group, so in the sake of fairness, not every Jewish person I mention necessarily subscribes to a faith in Judaism. So, what about entertainers who come from Jewish families? What about 'em? Just kidding! To me it's obvious. In America, many forms of media and entertainment are owned by Jews. Many artists, musicians, and entertainers are Jewish. My best friend Eric Davis who I mentioned in previous chapters is Jewish! So, don't sick the Anti-Defamation League on me or put me on the Jerry Springer show claiming I'm anti-Semitic.

Jewish Actors and Actresses:
Cary Grant -- Classical good looks and humor.
Alicia Silverstone -- Actress - Clueless, The Crush, The Babysitter,
    Batman, ect.
Barbara Streisand -- Singer and actress winner of two Oscars, four
    Emmys, nine Golden Globes, and other awards.
Mandy Patinkin -- Emmy & Tony award-winning actor, Dr. Jeffrey
    Geiger on TV's Chicago Hope.
Harrison Ford -- Actor: Raiders of the Lost Ark, Star Wars, American
    Graffiti, Witness, The Fugitive, ect.
Gwyneth Paltrow -- Oscar winning actress. Shakespeare in Love, The
    Royal Tenenbaums, Proof, ect.
William Shatner -- Captain James T. Kirk on the original Star Trek.
Natalie Portman -- Actress, Queen Amidala in Star Wars: The
    Phantom Menace.
Tori Spelling – Daughter of producer Aaron Spelling. Starred in his
    TV show Beverly Hills 90210 and also in various movies.
Winona Ryder -- Star of films like Heathers, Girl Interrupted, Little
    Women, ect.
Noah Wyle -- Actor, Dr. John Carter on TV's ER.
Michael Landon -- Little Joe Cartwright on TV's Bonanza.

Mark Frankel -- Actor in Sisters and Fortune Hunter.

Sarah Jessica Parker -- Actress on TV's Sex and the City, LA Story, ect.

Seth Green -- Television actor, Buffy the Vampire Slayer, Family Guy, ect.

Robert Downey, Jr. -- Actor in Less Than Zero, Chaplin, Short Cuts.

Paul Newman -- Academy Award winning actor and philanthropist.
    Musicians:

Itzhak Perlman -- Grammy-winning violin soloist. Played at President Barack Obama's inauguration.

Max Weinberg -- Drummer for Bruce Springstein and musical director for Conan O'Brien.

George Gershwin -- American composer of many vocal and theatrical works written in collaboration with his older brother, lyricist Ira Gershwin.

Scott Ian -- Guitarist for Anthrax. Born a Jew, but has a different faith now.

Adam Yauch -- Member of rap group the Beastie Boys. Converted to Buddhism.

Lenny Kravitz -- Hard rock singer and guitarist whose father is Jewish.

Herb Alpert -- Leader and trumpeter of the Tijuana Brass.

Comedians:

Jerry Lewis -- A comedian, actor, and philanthropist who teamed up with actor/singer Dean Martin in various movies.

Jerry Seinfeld -- Stand up comedian, TV show 'Seinfeld,' American Express commercials.

Milton Berle -- Comedian who pioneered comedy/variety on television.

Jack Benny -- Legendary radio and TV comic.

Directors and producers:

Steven Spielberg -- Director of films such as Saving Private Ryan, Schindler's List, Jurassic Park, E.T. ect.

Stanley Kubrick -- Director of 2001: A Space Odyssey, Clockwork Orange, The Shining, Full Metal Jacket, Spartacus.

Mel Brooks -- Film director, producer, actor: Blazing Saddles, Young Frankenstein, ect.

Woody Allen -- Film maker and actor: Annie Hall, Bullets Over Broadway, Mighty Aphrodite, Antz, ect.

Roman Polanski -- Director, screenwriter, actor: Rosemary's Baby, Macbeth, Chinatown, Tess, ect.

Ben Stiller – Director and actor: Seinfeld, SNL, Reality Bites, Something About Mary, The Cable Guy.
Aaron Spelling – Produced TV's: Beverly Hills 90210, Melrose Place, ect.
Oliver Stone -- Popular Director: The Doors, J.F.K., Heaven And Earth, Natural Born Killers.

Fashion designers:
Calvin Klein -- Famous clothing designer.
Ralph Lauren -- (Ralph Lipshitz) World famous fashion designer.
Levi Strauss -- Inventor of blue jeans.
Kenneth Cole – Renown fashion designer.

Wow! That was quite a list of those Jews eh? *smirk* Lastly, I am reminded of a more-direct relationship between faith and entertainment. Good News Communications is a Christian organization which produces *MOVIEGUIDE* , a magazine "founded to redeem the values of the entertainment industry." The organization has been active in Hollywood and in the White House to affect the content of entertainment.

It's advocacy arm is the Christian Film & Television Commission. The magazine reported in a "30 Anniversary" issue that in the 1960s the Protestant Film Office "shut down and within three years movies went from being 100% G-rated movies to 81% R-rated. However the magazine reported that that "in 2007 47.8% of movies released by Hollywood contained positive Christian content. The 81% of R-rated movies has dropped to 44%." Those are some interesting figures. In the sake of fairness, this author is curious about how they arrived at the numbers in the data they report. There are countless other examples of how faith and religion is related to entertainment. Every recognized religion or faith is not mentioned in this book, because there just simply isn't enough time or room in this volume to do so. Hopefully, readers can still appreciate the perspectives shared in this writing and can clearly see how faith and religion play important roles in entertainment.

THE FINAL CHAPTER

Happily Ever After...

This last chapter will close by recapping and summarizing everything in this book thus far. I want to encourage and inspire the world to never give up on its hopes and dreams. If I can come from a modest background filled with challenges and overcome having been paralyzed on the left side of my body, and still become a rock star, you can too! In spite of having a heavily scarred left arm with paralysis in my left hand, I have gone on to meet many wonderful and interesting celebrities and entertainers. My wonderful charismatic personality and incredible intellect combined with my years of experience and formal education make it impossible for folks to not want to know me better! *grin* Who cares how I look? I've got skills! My looks just happen to be a great bonus feature. *smirk*

The first chapter of this book shared about how it is necessary to have much wisdom and common sense in order to be successful in the entertainment industry. Perhaps, the most important thing I learned as a journalist writing about entertainment is that sometimes it's better "to be silent and to be thought a fool than to open one's mouth and remove all doubt." Just because I met someone and know some things about him or her doesn't necessarily mean I should tell those things to others. I fundamentally believe in respecting others and their privacy. This lesson was especially learned when I dealt with Southern rock and country musicians.

One of the early lessons I received regarding privacy came one night when I was a guest for former Allman Brothers guitarist and songwriter Dickie Betts. My good friend J.C. Haun, a great guitarist and musician in his own right, told me about how he was friends with Dickie Betts and had jammed with him some in Georgia. J.C. told me Dickie was coming to Knoxville with his band *Great Southern* and said I should come out to the show. I took J.C. up on his invitation and I came to Betts' show a few days later. I'm not sure who opened that show, but I believe it was my good friends *Left Foot Down,* whom I mentioned earlier because I spent some time in the studio with them and producer Scottie Hoglan. Anyhow, I didn't have any of Great Southern's CDs prior to that show, so I was not really familiar with the band. They played an incredible set that included Dickie leading the band in the tune "Midnight Rider," which he made famous with the Allman Brothers.

After the show, I learned the importance of privacy and trust between people working in the entertainment industry. J.C. Haun demonstrated this to me firsthand before and after the show while he and I were hanging out backstage talking. While we were chatting, Haun whispered to me "Hey man, I'm taking Dickie to his hotel after the show and I'm sneaking him out of the building. He's going to to ride in my truck. We're gonna sneak him out the back door surrounded by some bouncers. People will be waiting at his bus expecting him to be there, except he won't be. I'm going to pull my pickup around and we'll jump in and take off. DON'T TELL ANYBODY! If you do, I'll have to hurt you!"

Of course, I was cool and I got Dickie to sign my 1994 issue of *Guitar World Magazine* since he was on the cover. So, the end of the show came. J.C. didn't waste time playing around. He anxiously said "All right. Let's do this. James. You get the back door and sorta stand in the way like a fan, so we can slip past you." Just as planned, everything went off without a hitch. Haun drove his ragged old white Ford pickup around and parked it in front of Dickie's bus. It was inconspicuous indeed as it had a gun rack in the back window with Confederate flags and looked like any other common redneck truck one might find in East Tennessee. They quickly slipped out, jumped in the truck, and sped off to the hotel.

The next great band I learned some lessons from is Lynyrd Skynyrd. While I was living in Georgia back in 2005, I drove down to Florida for Mardi Gras at Universal Studios Themepark in Orlando. I went with an old friend whom will remain anonymous in this writing. It was the first and only time I have been there. Anyhow, it was really cool. My buddy and I stayed at a nice hotel and we had a great time on the rides and getting to experience Mardi Gras. Well, we got there and my bud got sick and had to take a bus back to the hotel that afternoon before Skynard had even played. So, that left me all alone to fight off chicks who wanted to hookup with the J-Dogg. *snicker*

Well, since my friend had a connection in the industry, I went about things in a very wrong way and tried to get to meet them. That's why my friend's name is not being mentioned. First of all, I apologize to Lynyrd Skynyrd for my behavior. I must have had "groupie fever" that day or something. Anyhow, I went to the ride for the movie *Twister*. While in there, I suddenly had to get out and go to the "great white thrown." So, I look over to my left and see an exit sign in red neon hanging from the ceiling. Feverishly, I worked my way through the crowd and back to the door.

Wow! I looked around and I couldn't believe it. I was backstage! "Holy crap! I am SO going to get to meet them! Universal would freak if they knew I was back here! I could get SO Bus-Ted!" I composed myself and calmly started strutting my way down the street in front of the stage after I turned to my left out of Twister. A few steps away from the Twister building there was a trailer that had some drinks and refreshments. Two guys were standing there chatting and I asked them what time Skynyrd was supposed to play and they told me. I thanked them and kept strolling by the stage toward the buses I was sure the band was in.

I got to just a few steps away from Lynyrd Skynyrd's bus and a White lady with shoulder-length brown hair stopped me and asked if she could help me. Naturally, I remained calm and showed her my pass and told her who I was. Unfortunately, that wasn't all I did. Let's face it, I was slimy that day. I told her about my friend's connection and I even whipped out a photo of me with someone Skynyrd had toured with that year. I stooped desperately low that day. What was I thinking? I mean, my bud was back at the hotel puking and all I could think of was meeting a legendary Southern rock band? The lady was the band's manager and she told me to come back in a few hours and I might get to meet the band, if they agreed.

Uh, okay. What was I to do? I mean, this was big time. Certainly it was, but I look back and realize that I could have killed my reputation as a journalist, which would have been TERRIBLE. I went to the restroom first and then I did what any other greedy poparazzi would do. I wondered over and bugged the sound guy during sound-check! *smirk* Oh, come on. Laugh with me. I had to learn my lesson! Well, while I was chatting with the sound tech, I began to ask him all sorts of stupid personal questions like "Do you know if Skynyrd's doing a meet n' greet with fans? I heard the band's guitarist left. Do you know who's gonna fill in for him tonight? I heard it might be Dickie Betts. Man, I bet this is going to be a pretty incredible show tonight. Do you have any idea how much Skynyrd charges to play at an event like this?" I know folks. I was out of line. I was terrible. The sound guy lit back with "Dickie Betts? Aw, no! What business is it of yours how much we're getting paid tonight? How much do YOU get paid every year? Buddy that's really personal information."

I apologized to the man and took a hike. I wondered around the park flirting with girls for a few hours and came back to speak with Skynyrd's manager. She cordially informed me that I could not meet Skynyrd, because nobody knew who I was. I had a fire inside of me for that moment that had just been peed on and snuffed out. I mean, I explained to her that I had called and left messages with some of Skynyrd's people and had emailed them prior to Mardi Gras requesting a meeting with them. I thought that I would have met them for sure, because after all my good name and reputation precede me in the South. Therefore, I went to Florida even though I did not have prior clearance with Skynyrd, because I figured I would have fun at Universal anyways regardless of whether or not I met them.

Well, Mardi Gras passed. Lynyrd Skynyrd played an incredible show and by my estimation there had to have been over 100,000 people there to hear them. They played all of their great classics, including my favorite "Simple Man." Well, I noticed something very special as I stood near the stage and watched when they began playing. "Oh snap! It's those two guys!" Yep, the two dudes I saw and asked what time Skynyrd would be playing were on stage playing with them! It was Billy Powell on the keyboards. The other guy was playing guitar that night, since the usual guitarist had just left the band. I think it might have been Johnny Winter. Anyhow, you can't make this stuff up! So, I sorta did get to meet two members of Skynyrd! I hope they don't mind me writing all of this down and publishing it. I have a lot of respect for all of them and I want to emphasize that I learned my lesson after that Mardi Gras. Famous or not, musicians are just people. They deserve the same respect and courtesy that you would normally give any person. Hopefully, these Southern rock legends will just laugh and grin real big when they read this and will not remember my poor behavior.

So, was I down about Skynyrd? Heck no! The next day I was still stoked and having a great time in Orlando! I woke up at about 10am and my anonymous friend was still green. My pal encouraged me and said "You go on James. I'm gonna crash here at the hotel and just take things easy. Go to the beach and have fun!" So, as I had already planned, I took a short drive over past Cape Canaveral to Cocoa Beach. Well, on the way there I stopped at a gas station to refuel and use the restroom. As I was waiting in line to pay the clerk, I noticed several young ladies traveling together. I particularly noticed one in line, because she was cute and had a mohawk.

Don't worry Katie (my wife), you don't need to shave your head! *grin* I was just young and single at the time. Anyhow, I started making small-talk with the punk rock chick and of course my charm and magnetism drew her friends over to me. I learned they were all college students who went to church together in Helen Georgia. What luck! I lived in Georgia and told them all about how I had training in Helen for my Department of Labor job! I explained that my bud got sick and was back at the hotel, so I was going to Cocoa Beach alone. "No your not," they said. "You can follow us there and hangout with us!" Score one for J Diddy! *smirk* Six girls! So, of course this story just keeps getting better, because after all I'm the greatest rock star to ever visit Cocoa Beach! We got there and we chatted for a few minutes and then had lunch together. After lunch, we all decided it was wise to let our food settle before getting in the water, so we all got into our bathing suits to relax and catch a few rays.

After fighting off rabid beach bunnies who tried to assault me with their sunblock (just kidding they were all nice young ladies), I noticed a cool band playing some smooth blues over at the cabana. I was instantly intrigued, because they had a guy on trumpet who also was playing keys and singing backup. He had a sweet-sounding horn. I walked over and said to him: "Hey man, I play a 1934 King, b-flat, Liberty trumpet. What kind are you playing?" He told me his trumpet was a Blessing and he said "Hey, I've got an extra mouthpiece if you wanna sit in."

I said "Sure!" and he handed me his trumpet and when the next song started I started jamming with them. The sax player motioned me over during the middle of playing and he whispered to me "Hey, play a solo." I walked up to the mic and began playing my solo. Oh no! The valves were sticking! "When was the last time this guy oiled his valves?! Stay cool," I thought. Of course I played it off as any true "playa" would and I just utilized my incredible skills to continue. By now, my lovely new entourage was gathered at the cabana being further impressed with the James man. *grin*

After the song ended, the manager of the cabana ran up to me and said "Oh my gosh! That was so awesome! Do you know who that was?" She proceeded to tell me that I had just jammed with *Ike and Tina Turner*'s bass player and with the drummer for *Three Dog Night*. After introducing me to them, she turned and pointed to members of Pat Benetar's band who were in the audience. That manager was very cordial and friendly and encouraged me to accept her invitation to come back and jam again sometime soon. After the music was over, of course, I got the band's contact info.

Well, this was enough excitement for one day I supposed. My new friends from Helen agreed and before we departed we exchanged emails. I emailed the girls a few times, but like any busy rock star, I soon lost contact with them. I have not seen or spoken to any of them, since we met that day. So, although things had not gone as planned on that trip to Florida, I learned three important lessons. They are: 1.) Life is short.

Enjoy it while you can. 2.) Always be respectful. 3.) Be poor while you're young, so you can still rock 'n roll when you're old!

The second chapter discussed how life in the entertainment industry isn't always glamorous. It reminded me of an event that happened one evening that I have not discussed yet. I went with my friend Eric Davis to see the rock band *Cracker* one evening at a club called Ziggy's in Winston-Salem, North Carolina. Eric had moved to North Carolina after we finished our master's degree program at UT, so that's why we were in North Carolina after I had moved to Georgia. Ziggy's was a small, but nice establishment. After the show I was hanging out with the band and struggling to chat with them, because I had a cold. Cracker's members all remembered me from other shows and articles I had written about them, so we were reminiscing about past events.

The band's lead singer told me "Brother. Don't try to talk. You need to stop man. You're gonna make yourself worse. Get yourself some hot tea and put honey in it. Drink that and get plenty of rest. I'm telling you what my own doctor has advised me prior to playing shows when I had a cold. You need to save your voice." Thanks Dr. David. I never forgot that little lesson and I'm using it right now as I write this passage, because I have a cold and a sore throat. Using the Lowery method, and saying plenty of prayers, I'm not worried about being glamorous and I know I'll feeling well soon. There were so many less than glamorous shows I can recall from my experiences. This one was one of the more memorable.

Hopefully, readers enjoyed my sharing some examples of my written work in Chapter 3. I wanted to give readers better ideas about the kinds of writing I do and about my experiences. The next chapter also shed some light on the kind of living this author has done in all of his "rock star" years. Then there's the photo chapter. The photos that made it into this book were the best. The ones that did not were because some folks were not cool enough to be included in this literary masterpiece! Just kidding... Seriously, there were some folks who decided during the process of this writing that they did not want to increase their coolness by being affiliated with James Hester. Those people are absolute losers! Their loss, my gain! *chuckle*

The last four chapters of this book solidified my argument that life as a rock star isn't always grand. Everyday television and Internet news programs broadcast videos of something heinous no matter how tasteless or offensive it may be to some, because they know it's entertaining. They only worry about it if it makes their ratings go down. Otherwise, everyone gets "biscuits for smut!" With the next chapter, I tried to gain credibility with my educated peers in the professional and academic world by citing some interesting numbers and statistics I found from various public sources, including the U.S. Department of Labor. With this book, I've wanted all along to have a broad demographic of readers. *smile*

During the final days and moments of writing for this book, the election race between Obama and McCain was plenty entertaining for this author. The controversy and slimy campaign tactics deployed by both the Democratic and Republican parties were at times quite obvious, which made watching the process all the more entertaining. Such was the inspiration for Chapter 8 of this piece. Because I am a man of faith, and I believe God blessed me with the ability to share my thoughts in writing, I saved the "God chapter" for last.

If readers will study the world's history, they might find quite often that God and the supernatural were common themes in entertainment. People have wanted to please gods or deities through the ages by using entertainment. Music, dances, theater, arts, and other various mediums have been used for centuries to entertain the "higher powers" of humanity. Those mediums have also served as countless outlets for expressions regarding God or the supernatural. Remember Gene Simmons' famous utterance "God gave rock 'n roll to you. Gave rock n' roll to you. Put it in the soul of everyone!"

The entertainment industry is filled with fame, glamour, and fortune, but it isn't always easy. There are a variety of highs and lows in the realm of entertainment. Hopefully, you have enjoyed the reflections shared in this book. A million other topics such as entertainment in education, theater, dance, martial arts, or a gazillion other things could have been discussed, but this author needs to save some things for other books. Perhaps, reflections on some of my personal experiences within the entertainment industry will help readers to think more broadly about the subject.

Since it took a considerable amount of time to process this book, publish it, and make it available for sale, I will make a few predictions for what to expect from entertainment in 2009:

1. Women will see increased recognition in professional sports and there will be more demand by consumers to have it aired on television. Things will be affected much by the law known as the *Lilly Ledbetter Fair Pay Act*. It was enacted by President Barack Obama. Girl power!
2. Due to a struggling U.S. economy, rock stars will become

increasingly clever in how they market themselves. They might drop their prices for a time or try to give consumers more for their money, but not for long. People in general feel that being entertained is absolutely essential for survival. No one will admit to having this feeling. Without a doubt, if folks start craving some fun, they will do whatever it takes to make themselves happy. Folks will sell blood plasma, trade food stamps, clone puppies, or sell their booger collections on eBay to satisfy their urges. There will never be a depression in the economy of entertainment.

3. Hey essay! Latino entertainment is where the money's gonna be! With the robust increase in Hispanic and Spanish-speaking people coming to America, it will be no surprise that the styles and trends in American and world entertainment will reflect this in all facets.

4. The CEOs and executives of major corporate entertainment companies should be prepared to answer to the American government any and all questions regarding the incomes and profits of their companies and employees. Similar to the federal government's bailout of The Big Three auto makers and mortgage companies nationwide, I predict the American government will want a slice of the pie. They will attempt to "stabilize the economy" by socializing entertainment. This is scary. It's an affront to civil liberties and basic human rights as we know them. Due to corporate greed and a disproportionate allocation of profits among company owners and their employees, the American economy will suffer. As a result some smooth-talking politicians will try to destroy capitalism and free-trade within the entertainment industry in order to try and help the overall economy.

5. More and more I see music and various other forms of entertainment being used as catalysts for peace globally. I believe music and sports will be used as safe mediums to encourage and bring about change in the world, particularly in African nations and in Middle Eastern countries. Bono and his Project Red is a good example of this. Al Gore and Kevin Wall's Live Earth series of global music concerts are another example of this.

Entertainment is like many other aspects of life in that it has moments when it is good as well as moments when it is just downright ugly. Be encouraged to bare your heart and soul for rock 'n roll. Shine like a star!